Case Studies in Criminal Justice Ethics

Second Edition

Michael Braswell
East Tennessee State University
Larry Miller
East Tennessee State University
Joycelyn Pollock
Texas State University

Long (

For information about this book, contact:
Waveland Press, Inc.
4180 IL Route 83, Suite 101
Long Grove, IL 60047-9580
(847) 634-0081
info@waveland.com
www.waveland.com

10-digit ISBN 1-57766-747-6
13-digit ISBN 978-1-57766-747-6

Printed in the United States of America

7 6

CONTENTS

PREFACE

The second edition of *Case Studies in Criminal Justice Ethics* continues to focus on personal, social, and criminal justice contexts in ethical decision making. For police officers, officers of the court, and corrections professionals as well as citizens, moral dilemmas not only challenge their personal values and professional ethics but also require them to make decisions often based upon ambiguous circumstances. It would be more desirable if ethical conflicts offered clear, black and white choices. More often than not, the fog of politics, personal bias, and past experiences also factor into one's decision making.

Case Studies in Criminal Justice Ethics is divided into four sections: Policing, Courts, Corrections, and Juvenile Justice. In addition to updating references for additional suggested reading, new cases have been added addressing such issues as prosecutorial politics, perceptions of terrorism, gun rights, domestic conflict resulting from post-traumatic stress syndrome, and the possibility of executing someone who may be innocent.

We believe these case studies add a personal, more realistic dimension to the challenges of making ethical choices and living more moral lives. As always, we welcome any suggestions about improving the book.

Michael Braswell
Larry Miller
Joycelyn Pollock

Acknowledgments

We want to acknowledge the value of the insights our students have given us as a result of our using these cases in classes we teach. In addition, we are appreciative of the suggestions from colleagues about new cases to include.

Our thanks to Linde Burkey for her help in updating references, and to our editor, Gayle Zawilla, for her help with this edition as well as the first. She has been a pleasure to work with.

INTRODUCTION

Ethics is a hot topic. It is mentioned in relation to politics, business, journalism, religion and criminal justice. Still, many people do not seem to have an accurate sense of what the term ethics means. A dictionary definition of ethics is:

> . . . a particular system of principles and rules concerning duty . . . rules of practice in respect to a single class of human actions. . . .

Using this definition, ethics could mean many things to many people, according to how it is applied. In essence, however, one could suggest that ethics is the study of human duty. But what are one's duties? Some are obvious and are inherent in our professional and personal roles. Members of society have a duty to both themselves and other members within that society to maintain certain standards of behavior. Statutes and laws, as imperfect as they may be, are derived from these standards. These formal rules of behavior guide us in our daily lives, but they are not the complete source of determining right or wrong. Most jobs and professions involve certain duties that are unique to that role and may not be shared by others. These form an additional network of rules and standards of behavior. In the criminal justice system, these professional duties sometimes carry the force of law, but not always.

Sometimes it is not clear whether a particular action is a duty or is in the realm of choice. The cases in this book have been designed to illustrate these possible disagreements in the professions that are related to the field of criminal justice. Ethical issues in criminal justice professions are inevitable, but they can be prepared for, and that is the purpose of this casebook. The cases have been drawn to help the reader learn to identify important issues, to provide a forum for discussion and, ultimately, to help the student learn how to resolve them.

How to Approach Ethical Issues

Ethics comprise the fundamental framework for how an individual lives his or her life and exists within society. Controversial issues such as abortion and capital punishment exist because individuals use different frameworks for deciding ethical issues, although sometimes two people can use the same framework or system and come up with different answers.

The two major categories of ethical frameworks are deontological systems and teleological systems. The major difference between these frameworks is that a deontological framework looks to the inherent nature of the act to determine goodness, while teleological frameworks are "end-oriented." They look at the effect of the act in order to determine whether it is good or bad. "The end justifies the means" is a phrase characteristic of a teleological ethical framework. Utilitarianism is one such framework. In this ethical system, what is good is that which benefits the many, and the needs of the majority outweigh the needs of the individual. A deontological ethical system, on the other hand, could never justify a bad act even if it resulted in a good end. According to this type of system, if something is wrong, it is always wrong and the end result is irrelevant. Immanuel Kant developed the best-known form of deontological ethics in his writings. According to Kant, what is good is that which conforms to the "categorical imperative." The "categorical imperative" is a stricture whereby everyone should do one's duty, treat each person as an "end" and not as a means (in other words, don't use people), and follow the rule of universalism, which states that you should act in a way that you would want everyone to act (Pollock 2012).

A very common source for helping to decide ethical issues is one's religion. Religions have always provided definitions of right and wrong and a compass for how to live one's life. Religious ethics don't fall neatly into either of the two categories above, although a religious ethical system is probably closer to a deontological system than a utilitarian one. We often focus on the differences between religions. It is true that religions have been the source of much strife throughout history, but they have also been a powerful source of good. In fact, there are many similarities between religions and what they define as good. In many cases, most religions would arrive at the same answer for an ethical dilemma.

Religion may not have the answers, however, when professionals face ethical dilemmas unique to their profession. In these cases, concepts such as duty, benefit to society, integrity, and loyalty are central. In many cases where individuals are troubled by ethical dilemmas, it is because there are values in conflict. For instance, a police officer who knows a fellow officer has engaged in wrongdoing must choose between the values of friendship and loyalty (to the organization and society).

Egoism is an ethical system that places the highest value on one's own self-interest. In any situation where an individual has a choice of behaviors, the choice would be to put one's own interests above anyone else's in society. Most philosophers reject this as a true ethical system. However, some philosophers suggest that humans can act in no other way. Even when someone does something that appears to be altruistic or engages in actions that appear to put others' interests above their own, it really is for their own good in some indirect way (i.e., satisfaction).

To resolve an ethical dilemma or evaluate an ethics issue, the first step should be to clearly identify all competing values. For instance, the crux of the issue in abortion is the value of life (of the fetus) over the value of personal privacy/rights (of the mother). In many professional situations, the value of duty conflicts with such values as personal pleasure or family or friendship. For instance, law enforcement officers are often asked to "fix tickets" or, in other ways, help individuals or family members with legal problems. Whenever there is a difficult choice, it is often because both values are important.

The second step is to evaluate all the possible choices one might make. It is possible that at first there seem to be only two, but upon further analysis a third or more options might be developed that would be better for all concerned. The third step would be to evaluate all these choices according to ethical frameworks.

To apply a utilitarian framework, one must determine the benefit of each choice of action for all concerned. This involves predicting the effects of such action for the future, admittedly a difficult proposition. Further, benefits and/or negative effects for all concerned should be considered, not merely the most directly relevant. The end result of such calculations should be the course of action that results in the most "good" for all concerned.

If one chooses a deontological system, typically universal rules will be applied (i.e., "don't hurt innocents," "treat everyone fairly," "always tell the truth unless you would endanger someone's life," and "don't do to someone else what you would not want done to yourself"). Once those rules are established, they define what is right and wrong, regardless of the potential good effects of a "bad" act (Pollock 2012; Braswell, McCarthy, & McCarthy 2011).

Thus, the steps of analysis are as follows:

1. Define all relevant values (and identify the conflicts).
2. Identify all possible courses of action.
3. Apply an ethical system to determine the "rightness" of each course of action.

While there are obviously distinct differences in the ethical issues that arise in law enforcement, the courts, and corrections, there are also many similarities. Those in the criminal justice field should never forget that their role involves a great deal of power and discretion. Whenever someone has discretion, there is the opportunity to use it unethically. In the case of criminal justice professionals, discretion occurs when a police officer chooses to give a ticket or a warning; when a prosecutor chooses whether or not to prosecute; and when a correctional officer makes a recommendation to the parole board concerning the release of an inmate or chooses to "write up" an inmate for rule breaking. These are but a few examples of the myriad ways in which criminal justice professionals exercise power. In any exercise of power, there must be the recognition of the ethical and unethical uses of power.

Ethics in Law Enforcement

Ethical issues in law enforcement illustrate the interplay of ethics and the law. Police officers don't arrest or ticket all people who violate the law, and they have the ability to resolve situations in a number of ways. Their choices reflect not only their training but also their individual ethics. Police officers often feel that the public unfairly scrutinizes them, and (justifiably) that the media tend to emphasize wrongdoing by police over any good works they accomplish. However, such scrutiny is warranted since they enforce the law. We see hypocrisy, for instance, when police officers expect different treatment for drunk driving, domestic violence, or other law violations, since they arrest others for these same acts. There is more room for dispute, however, when the issue is not a criminal violation but rather an ethical one. Should police officers be held to higher standards, for instance, in the area of cheating on one's spouse? Is it or should it be grounds for formal discipline when an officer has an extramarital affair? If so, why?

One of the areas ripe for ethical analysis is when police officers want to act illegally, or at least unethically, in order to secure a warrant or an arrest. This so-called "noble cause" corruption can be justified, perhaps, by utilitarianism, but never by any deontological ethics (Crank & Caldero 2010). Further, it is impossible to know if such actions really result in a good end for everyone, since we cannot predict the future. For instance, an officer who lies to get a warrant may end up ruining his or her own credibility and, therefore, may lose many more cases because the judge doesn't believe what the officer says.

Gratuities are a perennial issue in law enforcement. Should officers receive free or half-price meals? Who does it hurt? In order to find it wrong under utilitarianism, it would have to result in a net negative utility for all concerned. Are gratuities a harmless "perk" of the job, or do they result in a net negative effect for all concerned? Most departments have established policies on gratuities so there is the added element of whether or not an officer is violating a departmental rule. Even when one decides there is no harm in the gratuity, if taking it violates a departmental policy, that must also be considered, since it probably constitutes an inappropriate action.

Law enforcement is a difficult profession and every officer will, at some point in his or her career, face difficult choices that are outside the realm of the law or training. It is important, therefore, that all officers have a clear sense of right and wrong and have the ability to apply ethical analysis.

Ethics in Courts

How many jokes are there about lawyers? More importantly, why are they all condemnatory jokes that stereotype lawyers as liars, cheaters, and persons without scruples? It is an interesting conundrum, since attorneys are supposed to represent and uphold the sanctity of the law and be the guardians of rights. In essence, lawyers represent the reality that the law is not only "blind" but also can be subverted. The "letter of the law" may be different from the "spirit of the law," and whoever has the best attorney gets to define the "letter of the law." Good attorneys are experts at the technicalities of the law. At best, they make sure through the application and enforcement of all due process rights that the rights of individuals are not trampled by the state. At worst, they subvert justice through the manipulation of such rules. It has been said that as much as police officers hate defense attorneys, they are the first to demand their "union lawyer" in any situation in which they may face discipline. Those who are in the system know how important it is to have someone who can stand as a buffer between the individual and the power of the state. That someone is the defense attorney. Unfortunately, defense attorneys are only human, and overwork, burnout, personal bias, and other issues sometimes interfere with their performance.

Prosecutors, like police officers, may be tempted to engage in noble cause corruption, and it is just as damaging to due process when prosecutors engage in these actions. Innocent defendants can end up in prison or even on death row when prosecutors subvert procedural due process. The governor of Illinois felt so strongly about this issue that he was compelled to commute the life sentences of everyone on death row in 2002 because there was a possibility of actual innocence in a good portion of the cases. The possibility of innocent individuals being sentenced to death can often be traced to prosecutorial misconduct (Armstrong & Possley 2002). If their misbehavior is discovered, cases can be lost or overturned.

Noble cause corruption occurs when good people try to reach a good end by using questionable means; however, there are many other instances where individuals may be tempted to choose a course of action that can only be justified by self-interest. This is true in all the subsystems of the criminal justice process, but these incidents have special significance when the individual involved is a sworn officer of the court.

Ethics in Corrections

When someone's freedom is taken and they are placed in prison or jail, they do not give up basic human rights and the right to be treated ethically. Problems such as violence, health care, overcrowding, correctional officer brutality, and constitutional rights violations cannot be overlooked just because they occur within the walls of a correctional facility. The code of ethics of correctional professionals also seeks to control power and discretion and, in many ways, is very similar to law enforcement ethics. However, correctional professionals arguably must have even stronger ethics than police officers, because even the public may not care when they make bad choices.

Society often ignores the plight of inmates and feels that such problems do not concern them. Ethically, however, society's best interests are served by making sure that human rights are not discarded at the prison door. Treating inmates without any respect for their humanity is not conducive to reform, and reformed inmates are less inclined to become repeat offenders once they have finished serving their term.

Ethical issues in corrections involve the power to make decisions (e.g., whether or not to recommend probation or to file a violation report). It might involve using one's position for personal gain, or it may involve seeing a co-worker do so and then having to decide what to do about it. Every decision regarding a correctional client is clearly one that implicates the ethics of the decision maker. Although the public does not hold them in very high esteem, correctional professionals play an important role in the criminal justice system—one that can be all too easily forgotten in their day-to-day lives.

Ethics in Juvenile Justice

The way in which we as a society and criminal justice system respond to our troubled and delinquent youth could be viewed as indicative of our confidence in our country's future. In other words, our children are our future—future leaders, teachers, police officers, and (unfortunately) criminals. In some ways, the balance between juvenile justice, treatment, and rehabilitation is more delicate and more precarious than the balance regarding adult offenders.

Traditionally, law enforcement and the courts have attempted to take a more personal and "parental" posture with juvenile offenders, especially those guilty of status offenses such as truancy and underage drinking. Attempts have been made to divert troubled youth into more treatment-prone programs, away from the criminal justice mainstream. Currently, there seems to be a trend toward referring increasing numbers of juvenile offenders to adult court. While it is true that a teenage offender can be—and some are—as violent as an adult criminal, public and professional sentiment and beliefs also influence the politics of how juveniles are processed by law enforcement, the courts, and corrections. What is somewhat unclear is the extent to which current juvenile justice trends are influenced by popular notions based on media treatment and by high-profile cases, such as the Columbine shootings.

In a moral and ethical sense, what we do to our youth—even our most troubled and delinquent youth—we do to ourselves in the end. Do we emphasize crime prevention and early intervention? And when that does not work, do we try to divert juvenile offenders into more treatment-oriented and restorative justice programs, or do we remand them to adult courts and sentence them to adult prisons? Perhaps, more than with any other area in criminal justice, the way we respond is a fundamentally ethical matter.

Conclusion

Ethics involves applying philosophical, social, and political factors to discretionary decision making. The cases in this text deal with ethical dilemmas with which you may be confronted at some time in your professional career. The discussion of these moral and professional issues should help to clarify some important ethical principles. As you react to these cases, your own personal values, as well as related social and political factors, will most likely affect your decisions. Try to determine how you arrive at your decisions, and think about how your decisions will affect those around you.

Suggestions for Further Reading

Albanese, J. (2011). *Professional ethics in criminal justice: Being ethical when no one else is looking*. Upper Saddle River, NJ: Prentice-Hall.

Albert, E., Denise, T., & Peterfreund, S. (1984). *Great traditions in ethics*. Belmont, CA: Wadsworth.

Barry, V. (1985). *Applying ethics*. Belmont, CA: Wadsworth/ITP.

Braswell, M., McCarthy, B., & McCarthy, B. (2011). *Justice, crime and ethics* (7th ed.). Cincinnati, OH: Lexis/Nexis Anderson.

Braswell, M., Pollock, J., & Braswell, S. (2005). *Morality stories: Dilemmas in ethics, crime and justice*. Durham, NC: Carolina Academic Press.

Close, D., & Meier, N. (2003). *Morality in criminal justice: An introduction to ethics*. Belmont, CA: Wadsworth/ITP.

Dreisbach, C. (2008). *Ethics in criminal justice*. New York: McGraw-Hill.

Pollock, J. (2012). *Ethical dilemmas and decisions in criminal justice* (7th ed.). Belmont, CA: Wadsworth/ITP.

Souryal, S. (2010). *Ethics in criminal justice: In search of the truth* (5th ed.). Cincinnati, OH: Anderson.

Section I

ETHICS AND LAW ENFORCEMENT

Americans often have a love–hate relationship with law enforcement. On one hand, we recognize the need for fair, impartial enforcement of the laws and are quick to point out and demand explanations for police behavior we deem to be unethical. On the other hand, when it comes to following laws themselves, Americans tend to resent police interference, especially when we believe our own individual freedom has been restrained. It is not unusual to hear people voicing their disdain for police while at the same time supporting the notion that there is a need for more cops on the streets. American police officers tend to find themselves in a fish bowl—or, at times, on a video recording—and subsequently having to defend actions they thought were noble, or at least appropriate at the time. Because the police profession in America is a unique vocation that the public views with mixed emotions, it is always necessary for the police to practice ethical behavior and judgment.

The inclusion of police ethical decision making in training academies and academic institutions evolved from a growing frequency of complaints made against the police. These complaints ranged from media investigative reports of dishonesty and negligence, citizens capturing police misconduct on personal camcorders and smart phones, and citizens' general complaints about their encounters with the police. Below are some of the factors that influence police ethical decision making and contribute to the increase in frequency of public complaints against police officers.

1. Police are sometimes asked by others to ignore violations of the law for one reason or another.
2. Most police are visible in their uniforms and in their vehicles, making their actions—both good and bad—more noticeable to the public.
3. Enforcement of the law often creates resentment that sometimes becomes vindictive and personal.

4. Police officers are exposed to temptations not often found in other professions.
5. Officers in the field usually work without direct supervision, a fact that creates additional opportunity for misconduct and unethical practices.
6. The public tends to be more critical of police because the police are expected to exhibit a higher level of ethical and professional conduct than others. When they do not exhibit this higher degree of good conduct, complaints may ensue.
7. The nature of police work occasionally attracts persons who have antisocial or aggressive tendencies, which creates a need for psychological screening.
8. During police contacts emotionally volatile situations are frequently encountered (e.g., arrests, interviews at crime scenes, and so on). Intense emotions can obscure reason and judgments of both police officers and citizens.

It is often said that nothing is wrong with the police profession that is not wrong with the entire American society. After all, law enforcement does not exist in a vacuum but represents a cross-section of the community they serve. Therefore, the morals, attitudes, culture, and prejudices that exist in a community are mirrored in the local police agency. Because most decisions made by the police are discretionary, officers may find themselves in situations with no clear policy guidelines or enlightened supervision. If an officer takes action, will he or she be ostracized? If they don't take action, will police officers be criticized for failing to do their duty?

Most recruits enter the police profession with an idealistic and noble attitude. Most believe they will be enforcing the law, protecting the public, saving lives, making arrests for breaches of the peace, and keeping dangerous criminals off the streets. While such an idealistic attitude has merit, many officers change to a more realistic attitude after a relatively short time on the job. Tickets are sometimes "fixed," and the courts often treat celebrities and prominent citizens too generously. Officers become frustrated when they see the fruits of their labors spoiled by injustices within the system. Most police officers tend to adapt to the system and work as best they can under the constraints of their job. Others may resort to making sure the wheels of justice turn in their favor by using unethical practices. A few might resort to all-out corruption, getting what they can from what they perceive as a corrupt system.

The emphasis on police ethics is often thought of as just another way of trying to control police misconduct, but the issues involved are much more complex than that. While police misconduct is certainly a large part of police ethical decision making, it does not consider the myriad situations and ethical dilemmas with which an officer may be faced. Some actions a police officer takes may not be construed as misconduct but still may be unethical. At other times, an ethical decision may be considered misconduct. For example, a police officer who transports a badly injured child to the hospital rather than waiting for the ambulance to arrive may have made an ethical decision to save a life. However, that same decision may have violated department policy or even state law. A police officer who plants evidence on a known drug dealer in order to firm up a conviction and get a dangerous offender off the streets is, in fact, committing a crime as well as acting unethically. The officer who perceives his or her actions as noble actually considers him- or herself more ethical than a flawed justice system that might let such an offender off on a "technicality."

Most researchers have supported the need for improved training and education in the area of police ethics. Scholars have recognized a number of actions police agencies can incorporate to improve police ethical decision making within their ranks:

1. Improved selection and screening techniques for persons entering police service, especially those selected for leadership positions.
2. Increasingly stringent personnel requirements, such as advanced education and formal training, including the encouragement of higher education for in-service police ethics.
3. Basic research and development in police organizations, policy-setting techniques, and community attitudes toward the police.
4. Policy guideline formulation as well as training in policy application and practice within the department.
5. More control over discretionary decision making by police officers.
6. Facilitating a change in citizens' perspective of the police by developing supportive services within the community as well as in the department.
7. Increased review of police actions by independent agencies and media representatives knowledgeable of the police profession.

It is generally understood that police ethical decision making encompasses a broad range of police behavior including corruption, discrimination, violation of civil rights, and other misconduct. There are degrees of ethical decision making from acceptable behavior to outright corruption and malpractice. And, while the "slippery-slope" doctrine may have some following, it appears these degrees of ethical decision-making dilemmas do have boundaries for most officers. An officer may go from accepting free coffee at the local restaurant to accepting a bribe to ignore a minor infraction of the law. However, that same officer may draw the line at taking a major payoff from a drug lord in exchange for advance warning before an impending raid. So, like the rest of our society, the police may walk the straight and narrow path yet may still deviate from it, from time to time bending the rules, or may select the crooked path. However, as most researchers have observed, proper selection and training can help assure that officers will choose the proper path in their ethical decision making.

Suggestions for Further Reading

Alderson, J. (1998). *Principled policing: Protecting the public with integrity.* Winchester, MA: Waterside Press.

Alpert, G. P., Dunham, R. D., & Stroshine, M. S. (2006). *Policing: Continuity and change*. Long Grove, IL: Waveland Press.

Barker, T., & Carter, D. (1994). *Police deviance* (3rd ed.). Cincinnati, OH: Anderson.

Barlow, D. E., & Barlow, M. H. (2000). *Police in a multicultural society.* Long Grove, IL: Waveland Press.

Braswell, M. C., McCarthy, B. R., & McCarthy, B. J. (2011). *Justice, crime and ethics* (7th ed.). Cincinnati, OH: Anderson.

Braswell, M. C., Miller, L., & Whitehead, J. (2010). *Human relations and police work* (6th ed.). Long Grove, IL: Waveland Press.

Caldero, M. A., & Crank, J. P. (2010). *Police ethics: The corruption of noble cause* (3rd ed.). Cincinnati, OH: Anderson.

Chevigny, P. (1997). *The edge of the knife: Police violence in the Americas.* New York: The New Press.

Cohen, H., & Feldberg, M. (1991). *Power and restraint: The moral dimension of police work.* New York: Praeger.

Delattre, E. (2006). *Character and cops: Ethics in policing* (5th ed.). Washington, DC: AEI Press.

Dunham, R. G., & Alpert, G. P. (2009). *Critical issues in policing* (6th ed.). Long Grove, IL: Waveland Press.

Fyfe, J., Greene, J. & Walsh, W. (1999). *Police administration* (5th ed.). New York: McGraw-Hill.

Heffernan, W., & Stroup, T. (Eds). (1985). *Police ethics: Hard choices in law enforcement.* New York: John Jay Press.

Kleinig, J. (2002). Rethinking noble cause corruption. *International Journal of Police Science & Management, 4*(4), 287–314.

Lynch, G. (Ed.). (1999). *Human dignity and police: Ethics and integrity in police work.* Springfield, IL: Charles C. Thomas.

Neyroud, P., & Beckley, A. (2001). *Policing, ethics and human rights.* Devon, England: Willan Publishing.

Perez, D. & Moore, J. (2002). *Police ethics: A matter of character.* Belmont, CA: Wadsworth.

Swanson, C., Territo, L., & Taylor, R. (2007). *Police administration: Structures, processes, and behavior* (7th ed.). Upper Saddle River, NJ: Prentice-Hall.

1

Homegrown Terrorism

"I don't know why you're hassling us. It's his kind that flew that plane into the World Trade center and killed *real* Americans! Who knows what he and his friends were planning to do next?" the sixteen-year-old boy protests.

"Yeah, my Daddy says they won't rest until all Americans are dead, and besides, they worship the devil!" his fifteen-year-old sidekick adds.

You look at your patrol partner, Mary Bivins, before responding to the two youths you have just arrested for assault and vandalism. After a deep breath, you return your gaze directly to the youths.

"You two brave patriots beat up a seventy-five-year-old American citizen and tried to burn his house down. Mr. Hafiz and his wife have lived in this neighborhood for the last twenty years. In fact, one of his sons is a police officer over in the twelfth precinct, and he has another son who works as a fireman up in Albany. You two boys are in a whole lot of trouble."

Mrs. Unger, the fifteen-year-old's mother, brings coffee into the living room where the two boys, their parents, and the two police officers are sitting.

"How is Mr. Hafiz?" she inquires.

Officer Bivins's response is to the point. "He has a concussion and two broken ribs—"

Mr. Evans, the sixteen-year-old's father, interrupts Officer Bivins impatiently: "C'mon, officers! They were just being rambunctious teenagers who got carried away. I'll make sure they apologize to the Hafiz family, and us and the Ungers will see that their house is repaired. Who knows where kids get the crazy ideas they have these days? They didn't mean no serious harm."

Putting the coffee cup down, you look at the Evans and Unger families.

"I can't say what your sons' intentions were or where they got the idea to do what they did. The fact is, they committed a serious assault and caused extensive property damage. Officer Bivins and I will have to take them to the juvenile detention center. You can try to arrange to have them released to your custody tomorrow until the court hearing."

You and your partner ride in silence on the way back from the detention center. Finally Mary speaks: "I can't believe those parents, especially Mr. Evans."

"Yeah," you respond, "I'm not so sure they shouldn't have been arrested as well."

Questions for Discussion

1. How can parents instill, even if unintentionally, racial, ethnic or religious prejudice in their children?
2. Is it difficult to maintain an unbiased perspective and sense of balance when acts of terrorism result in the loss of innocent lives? Should the police and/or the courts take this into consideration under circumstances like the one outlined above?
3. How can schools, police, and other social and government institutions educate and help prevent such acts against persons of different ethnic or racial backgrounds?
3. What would be a just outcome to this case?

2

Park Place

"Jimmy, if I catch you speeding one more time, I'm going to call your Daddy, and you know what that will mean," Officer Smith says as he hands the young man his third warning ticket in the last three months. "Doing sixty miles an hour in a school zone is unacceptable!"

"Yes sir, Officer Smith. I promise I'll be more careful in the future," Jimmy replies. Jimmy's girlfriend, Lola, lights a cigarette and the two teenagers drive away to the sound of heavy metal music blaring from the car stereo.

Sergeant Bill Smith, your new partner, returns to the cruiser, stashes his clipboard, and turns on the ignition.

"You ready for a coffee break? They've got great latte down at the Croissant and Thistle coffee shop."

"Sure," you reply.

You order a hot chocolate while Bill asks for a croissant and latte. Once you get your drinks and food, Bill steers you to a quiet table in the corner.

"How's your hot chocolate?" Bill inquires. "Fine," you answer.

Swallowing the last of his croissant, your new partner clears his throat. "Jack, I know Park Place must seem like a different world from the Southside precinct, and I guess in a way it is. We do things differently here. Most of the folks are well-connected professionals—doctors and such. You might say our role is more supervision and less enforcement, like the young man I just pulled over for speeding. Jimmy Hamm's father is Reverend Dennis Hamm, senior pastor of a large, influential Baptist church. In fact, the mayor, a state senator, and four of the city commissioners attend his church. Jimmy's not a bad kid, just spoiled—although next time I catch him speeding, I *will* call his father. He knows if I talk to his father, I'll tell him about that white trash he's dating. And he knows that won't sit none too well with his father. If you have any questions, feel free to put 'em on the table."

"Well Sergeant," you begin, "this precinct is a lot different than the one I came from. In Southside, Jimmy would have gotten a ticket the first time we caught him. I know it's a lower income area, but I thought 'the law is the law.'"

"It is. It is, Jack," Bill says with a chuckle. "The law is the law. It's just that we apply it differently here than you did in Southside. You'll be fine. I'll bet they didn't have hot chocolate made with real chocolate down in Southside."

As you walk to your car after the shift is over, you reflect on your first day in Park Place. It was definitely easier duty than where you had come from. Still, the knot in your gut lets you know you are uneasy about your new partner's approach to law enforcement.

Questions for Discussion

1. What is the officers' duty? Can duty be defined differently based on who broke the law?
2. If it's unethical to let Jimmy go, what if the offender were a poor young mother whom you know doesn't have the money to pay a fine?
3. If we don't enforce the law all the time, against everyone, what are ethical criteria? What are unethical criteria?

3

Room at the End of the Hall

You have just showered and changed into civilian clothes. You think to yourself that, for a training officer, Sergeant Womack is all right. You have learned a lot from him during the last six weeks. Being a rookie police officer has gone much more smoothly than you thought it would. Finishing the last of your umpteenth cup of coffee, you can't help but overhear the sergeant and the afternoon shift dispatcher discussing several neighborhood calls complaining about a weekend fraternity party on Elm Street.

You say to the sergeant, "Sarge, I used to be a member of that fraternity when I was a criminal justice student at the university. I'd be happy to stop by on my way home and check it out. College boys can get a little out of control at times. I don't mind making a visit and getting them to quiet things down."

Sergeant Womack looks at the dispatcher and then turns to you.

"OK, Mike. Just be sure if there is any trouble, you call me pronto."

"You got it, Sarge," you respond, chuckling to yourself and remembering your wild and crazy times at the fraternity house.

Parking your truck by the street in front of the fraternity house, you can see the situation is about what you expected. You quickly herd those persons partying in the yard into the house and announce to all, pulling your badge, to hold things down since the neighbors are complaining to the police. Your voice has a firm but friendly tone to it and the partygoers, with a couple of minor exceptions expressed by several intoxicated brothers, generally comply with your request. You ask one fairly responsible-looking student in a fraternity sweatshirt where Ed, the organization's president, is, and he directs you to the last room on the right upstairs.

Entering the room, you observe seven or eight male students all watching some kind of activity in the corner of the room. Several are shouting encouragement while the rest are drinking beer and watching in silence. The observers are so enthralled with what is going on that they don't even notice your presence as you work your way through the crowd to see what is going on. You stop in your tracks. There on a bed is a male student having intercourse with a girl. Next to the bed is another male student zipping his pants up. You cannot tell what state of mind the girl is in. She seems intoxicated and confused, and perhaps even somewhat frightened. Not exactly sure what to do, you pull your badge and tell everyone to step outside the room and not leave the house. You stop Ed and two males who were obviously having sex with the girl and have them remain in the room. Ed, the fraternity president, has by this time recognized you. The girl starts to cry quietly, the two males become very nervous, and the rest of the observers quickly vanish from the room.

"Mike," begins the president, extending his hand to you, "We were just having some harmless fun."

"I'm not so sure about that, Ed," you reply, pulling out a notepad and pen and ignoring his extended hand. You direct Ed to take the two males to an adjoining room and wait for you there. You turn back to the girl, who has by now managed in some fashion to get dressed. You ask her what was going on. All she can manage between quiet sobs is that she is scared and that her name is Yvonne. You try to encourage her that everything will be all right and ask her to remain in the room while you question Ed and the other two males next door. As you leave the room, you look up and see Dr. Madge Mullins, assistant dean of students, walking toward you. You know her from your days as a student.

"Mike, I got a call from a student downstairs who works in my office. What's going on here?"

You quickly explain the situation to her as you know it. You can tell from the look on her face that she is both concerned and agitated.

"Mike, you said the girl's name was Yvonne? I've dealt with her before. She doesn't have the best reputation on campus. This is a university matter and I will guarantee you that this situation will be handled in an appropriate manner. There is no need for us to further embarrass this girl or the university, for that matter. You know what happens when these things get in the paper."

You carefully consider what Dean Mullins is saying. You also remember your sergeant's parting words. Do you let her take care of the situation or do you call Sergeant Womack?

Questions for Discussion

1. What is Mike's duty?
2. Does the fact that the girl in this situation has a "reputation" make a difference?
3. What would be a legally responsible and morally just outcome to this particular case?

4

A Victim of Rape?

You are responding to a sexual assault call. The report is from an apartment complex in a poor section of the city. The only information you were given is an apartment number, which was relayed to the dispatcher by a neighbor of the victim.

As you approach the entrance to the apartment, a woman swings the door open and says, "It's about time you showed up."

You recognize the woman as Janice, a prostitute who works the neighborhood. Jokingly, you ask if she has been raped. Janice sneers at you and says no. Leading you inside the apartment she introduces you to a young lady sitting on a couch, crying. "She's the one that was raped," Janice says to you. You ask her if the young lady is a friend and she tells you that she is. You also ask Janice if the young lady is a prostitute. Janice indignantly responds that the girl is not a prostitute.

The young lady is dressed in a short, see-through nightgown. She does not appear to be injured physically. The apartment does not appear to reflect any recent violent actions. You begin to wonder if Janice is telling the truth about the girl not being a prostitute. You see no evidence of a husband or children living in the apartment with the girl. You have worked in this neighborhood for quite a while and have begun to realize how young girls living alone in apartment buildings like this one make their living—as prostitutes.

"What's your name?" you ask the girl. "Ann . . ." the girl answers as she looks up at you and wipes the tears from her face.

You ask Ann if she knows her assailant and she gives you a description, indicating that she knows his first name. "Pete, that's the only name I know him by," she explains.

"Then you do know him?" you ask with some degree of skepticism.

"He's just an acquaintance," Ann snaps back.

You are now becoming more convinced that Ann is a prostitute and that Pete was probably a nonpaying customer.

"Did Pete rape you here?" you ask while looking around the apartment.

"In the bedroom," Ann responds.

"Naturally," you think to yourself as you survey the bedroom.

"What do you do for a living?" you ask Ann.

Ann explains that she just moved to the city a few weeks ago and is looking for a secretarial position.

"Well, Ann, to be completely honest, this doesn't look good," you explain. "First, you say you're raped by some guy that you are acquainted with and only know that his name is Pete. Second, your apartment doesn't appear to have been broken into by force. Third, you don't have any bruises or cuts on your body that would indicate a man assaulted you."

"Well, what the hell would you do if a guy had a damned knife at your throat?" Ann shouts at you angrily.

You try to keep your composure as you say, "I don't mean to be an asshole about this, but if I went out and arrested this Pete guy, it would only hurt you. A trial jury would laugh you out of the courtroom. The jury would have you pegged as a prostitute by the time the defense attorney was through with you."

You continue by pointing out to Ann that it would probably be a waste of time if she went to the hospital for a checkup in that all the reports and procedures that would have to be done would more than likely be thrown out of court.

Ann begins to cry again and tells you to forget the whole matter.

Walking out the door, you turn and tell Janice to be sure that her new apprentice gets payment in advance the next time. She responds with a glare.

Two days later at roll call your sergeant makes an announcement. "Men, we've apparently got a rapist on the loose in the northeast section of the city. All we know is that he tells his victims his name is Pete. This guy raped a minister's wife last night, and the boss wants us to catch him before the media come down on us."

As the sergeant describes Pete and the M.O. he uses, you remember the rape call you investigated two days ago. The description and the M.O. match the statement Ann had made to you. You are now faced with forgetting about the incident with Ann or returning to her apartment to obtain a statement. You realize you probably made a mistake treating Ann's rape as lightly as you did. If you go back now, she will probably be uncooperative, and your supervisor will want to know why you didn't complete the investigation in the first place.

Questions for Discussion

1. Why did the police officer in this case form inaccurate assumptions about the victim?
2. What should he do once he realizes his mistake?

5

Different Choices, Equal Protection

"You folks need to settle your differences and get along," Sergeant Waddell mumbles as he leaves the apartment with you trailing behind him. The sergeant, a 30-year veteran, switches on the ignition of the cruiser and continues, half-talking to you and half-talking to himself.

"I don't know what the world's coming to! Two men living together like that. It just ain't natural. It's tough enough dealing with the Saturday night husband-and-wife drunks without having to try to calm down the likes of them. They like to call themselves gay, but from the looks of that smaller one, it don't look like he was having too gay of a time. Looked like that bigger feller whipped up on him. Besides, him being as thin as he was, I wouldn't be surprised if he didn't have AIDS. I'll tell you one thing, I was glad to get out of there. Who knows what kind of germs was in their apartment?" Lighting a cigarette, he turns to you. "I bet they didn't teach you how to deal with those kind of people in college."

You pause before you respond, not wanting to offend the sergeant, who is also your training officer. "We were taught that it would be difficult and challenging when dealing with the homosexual community—because of AIDS, our own biases and prejudices, and a lot of the myths that are going around."

"Myths, my ass," Sergeant Waddell interrupts. "That AIDS disease will kill you stone-cold dead. I don't trust the government. You can't tell me you can't catch that stuff from mosquitoes either. Who knows how you can catch it? All I know is I want to wash my hands."

"Well, I would agree that there are a lot of questions," you reply. "But our professors always reminded us that every citizen was entitled to equal protection under the law, regardless of their sexual preference. I was taught that I was to treat them professionally, just as in any domestic disturbance. It seems to me that we should have done something besides just telling them to quiet down and get along with each other. I mean, we should have arrested the big guy just like we would have done it if was a spousal abuse case."

Pulling into the McDonald's parking lot, the sergeant turns once more to you. "Simpson, you're a good kid and I believe you will make a fine officer. But you need to remember that the classroom is one thing and the real world is another. I don't hate that kind of people, but they made their bed and now they'll have to lie in it. I don't know what else we could have done. They weren't married and, even if they were, I don't believe it's legal in this state. We couldn't take the little guy to a spousal abuse shelter, they'd laugh their asses off at us. And I don't think the domestic violence law covers people like that anyway. Why don't you go order us a couple of black coffees to go while I wash my hands?"

Waiting on the coffee, you reflect on Waddell's words. He is a respected veteran police officer and you understand his uneasiness. You feel it, too. You also remember the look of fear and helplessness on the face of the battered guy, Eddie, who called the police. One part of you wants to go back to check on him and do something, even if it means arresting the other guy for domestic violence. Another part of you wants to stay on Sergeant Waddell's good side. After all, he is your training officer. What are you going to do?

Questions for Discussion

1. Should same-sex relationships be covered under domestic violence and spousal abuse laws?
2. What should the officer do in this case?

6

A Christmas Wish

You are a young police officer in a midsize city. It is Christmas Eve and you have just finished your shift. It began raining late in the afternoon and, with the exception of some last-minute shoppers, things have been pretty uneventful. The cold rain began to change to ice when you got off at eight. You are on your way home to be with your family when you see a homeless woman struggling with a cardboard box near an alleyway. You shake your head and find yourself feeling sorry for the woman. She appears to be about the same age as your mother. You know your spouse and son are expecting you home, but you don't want to leave this woman out in the cold rain. All she has to protect her from the cold is the cardboard box. After some thought, you turn your patrol car around to see if you can help.

When you walk up to the woman's box, she starts yelling at you.

"Get away . . . leave me alone! Why don't you chase criminals or something instead of bothering me? I've not done anything."

You explain that you are just trying to help and ask if she would get into the patrol car so you can talk with her. She begins screaming at you again.

"You're not taking me to jail. I haven't done anything. Don't bother me. Leave me be!"

You become frustrated. Here you are, standing outside in the cold rain, trying to help someone who does not want your help. As you are being screamed at by the woman, you begin to think once more about your spouse and son waiting for you at home. You even begin to wonder if you did the right thing in stopping.

"Why am I doing this?" you ask yourself. "I need to get home and put my son's bike together. He'll be going to sleep soon, and I want to get a chance to play with him a while before he's off to bed."

You decide that you cannot leave the woman out in the icy cold. You get into your patrol car and ask the dispatcher to contact the shelter to see if they can take the woman. As you are waiting for the dispatcher to call you back, you notice that the woman's cardboard box will not hold up much longer in the rain. You know you must do something and wish you could make her understand that you just want to help.

"Unit 27, the shelter says they are full but they may be able to make room for her. You'll have to transport, though. By the way, the weather information says it's going to be in the low teens tomorrow and below zero tonight with the windchill around minus fifteen degrees," the dispatcher says.

As you get out of your car, the wind hits your face and already feels much colder than it was before. You approach the woman, and she begins to yell at you again.

"Why can't you cops leave me alone? No wonder people call you pigs!"

"Look, lady, I am trying to help you. If you don't come with me to the shelter you'll probably freeze to death out here," you respond, trying to convince her.

The woman begins to curse you and spit at you. You realize she will never go to the shelter voluntarily.

"OK, lady, have it your way. Stay out here and freeze if you want to. I don't need this abuse. Have a very merry Christmas," you say with disgust as you walk away.

As you leave, you advise the dispatcher that the woman will not go to the shelter with you. You also ask the dispatcher to make sure the next shift patrol in this zone checks on her. As you hang up the microphone, you know the next shift will probably not have time to check on the woman. After all, it is Christmas Eve and, with a skeleton force working the next shift, they'll probably have their hands full answering other calls.

The time you spend at home allows you to forget about the woman. Your spouse kept dinner warm for you, and your son was eager for you to come home. He was so excited about Christmas. As you put him to bed, he said his prayers and asked that everyone in the family be together, safe and warm on Christmas. Your son's prayers make you think about the woman you left out on the street. You can hear the wind howling outside. You wonder how she is faring.

Questions for Discussion

1. Why would a homeless person refuse help from a police officer on a cold, rainy night?
2. Should you force the homeless woman in this case to seek shelter, or should you abide by her wishes to be left alone?
3. Are there any other alternatives?

7

Fringe Benefits

Climbing into the passenger side of a patrol car, you position yourself beside your new partner, Bert Thompson. You have been working in the city jail as a detention officer since you graduated from the police academy three weeks ago. It is standard policy for your department to have new officers work inside prior to patrol duty.

"Name's Bert. Bet you're glad to get out of jail duty and onto some patrol," Bert remarks with a big grin.

"Sure am. My name's Warren," you reply.

"OK, Warren, let's go fight crime," says Bert as he pulls out of the parking lot. After driving a short distance, Bert breaks the silence.

"Warren, it's almost eight-thirty and looks like our side of town is pretty slow this morning. How about a cup of coffee?"

"Fine, there's a coffee shop over there," you point out.

"No, no, not that place. Prices higher than a cat's back. I know this doughnut place just up the road," Bert says.

Bert pulls into a franchised coffee and doughnut shop and tells you to wait in the cruiser and monitor the calls from headquarters.

"How do you like your coffee, Warren?" Bert asks as he steps out of the car.

"Black," you respond.

You see Bert through the large windows of the doughnut shop joking with one of the waitresses as he orders the coffee. You notice the waitress handing a large bag to Bert and begin to wonder how much coffee he bought.

"What did you do, buy out the whole place?" you ask as Bert climbs back into the cruiser.

"Well, I thought a few doughnuts wouldn't hurt along with our coffee," Bert says as he takes coffee cups from the bag.

"How much I owe you for mine?" you ask Bert.

"Not a thing. This was on the house, if you know what I mean," Bert responds with a grin.

"They told us at the academy we weren't supposed to take gratuities or anything like that," you state, trying to remain objective.

"Look Warren, on the salaries we make and the type of work we do, it's not a gratuity to take an occasional free ride. Most merchants in the community enjoy giving the cops a free meal or a discount now and then—it makes them feel like they can contribute. When we eat lunch today we'll get that for free, too, or at least at a discount. Restaurant owners like to see cops in their establishments. It makes for good business."

"Yeah, but what if they want something in return?" you ask.

"Warren, in twelve years of police work I've had maybe two or three ask me for a favor. Anyway, they weren't big things—fixing tickets, and stuff like that," Bert responds patiently.

Bert's argument seems pretty convincing. After all, Bert says that everyone in the department does it to some extent, including the chief.

That night, as you prepare to go to your night class at the university, you check your work schedule for the next month and notice that you will be rotating to the 3–11 shift in three weeks.

Rotating onto the afternoon-evening shift poses a problem for you. You are working on an associate's degree at the university and are going to two night classes a week. Rotating to the 3–11 shift means that you will miss two weeks of classes. It is too late in the semester to drop the classes without penalty, so you decide to talk with the instructors concerning your problem.

Your first instructor, Dr. Whitaker, was very understanding and provided you with a research paper assignment to make up for the lost time. You had one more instructor to contact.

"Dr. Rowland, I'm sorry but I've been switched over to an evening shift and I'll have to miss the next couple of classes. Is there anything I can do to make up the work that I'll miss?"

"Warren, your grades have been very good, but you know how I feel about student absenteeism. Unless you can work something out with your supervisor so that you can come to class, I would suggest that you withdraw from the course or face a serious grade reduction," Dr. Rowland suggested.

You did not want to withdraw because you currently have an A in the course and the semester will be over in six more weeks. You decided that you would talk with your lieutenant and see if you can get your off-days changed.

"No way, Warren. You know the policy. Unless there's illness or an emergency, we can't change the schedule. It would screw up the whole shift," the lieutenant explains.

A couple of days later you receive a phone call from Dr. Rowland.

"Warren, this is Tim Rowland. Did I wake you up?"

"No, Dr. Rowland, today is my day off. By the way, I guess I'll try to stick with the class and take my chances. I wasn't able to get my work schedule altered, but I figure I can take a C if I make all As and miss a couple of classes," you explain.

"Warren, I'm not calling about that but, well, I need a favor. My son got his third speeding ticket in a year yesterday, and I was wondering if there was anything you could do to help."

"Well, I don't know, Dr. Rowland. Who gave your son the ticket?" you ask reluctantly.

"An Officer Thompson. Listen, if you can help, I would certainly appreciate it. I believe I could work out your class problem and give you a final grade for the work you have already accomplished. I believe you have an A in the course up to now," Dr. Rowland adds.

"Officer Thompson" is your partner, Bert. It would be very easy to persuade Bert to fix the ticket and alleviate your problem with the class. By fixing the ticket you would be guaranteed an A for the course. On the other hand, you consider yourself a straight cop and not one to take payoffs. You wonder if it would be corrupt to fix the ticket. It does not really seem like such a big deal. Still, there was no mistaking what the instructor at the academy said.

Questions for Discussion

1. If you refuse to fix the ticket, what course grade are you likely to receive?
2. Can you seek help from other places?
3. Where should an officer draw the line concerning acceptance of gratuities?

8

The Transmission of Justice

"If there is anything you can do to help, Officer Jenkins, I would really appreciate it."

After assuring Mr. Arnaud that you would see what you could do, you hang up the phone and stare out the window, watching the September rain fall.

Six months ago, Mr. Arnaud's seventeen-year-old son, Tony, had been implicated in a car-stereo theft ring. As a veteran detective, it had always been your policy to divert juveniles from the justice system whenever possible and to handle each situation as informally as possible. Since there was only nonspecific hearsay evidence against Tony by one of the boys who got caught breaking into a car, you worked out a pre-trial diversion arrangement with the Assistant DA for Tony to do two months of volunteer work at the local boys and girls club and to receive counseling. He agreed, and two months later his record was expunged. Tony seemed like a good kid. He made decent grades and liked to fish. You remember thinking to yourself, "A kid who likes to fish can't be that bad."

After the first snowfall, the transmission in your SUV had broken down and needed repair. "Transmissions R US" had kept your truck for two weeks and had finally called to tell you it was ready. You had stopped by the credit union to do the paperwork for a short-term loan—SUV transmission work was always expensive! When you had attempted to pay the clerk for the repair, she asked you to wait for a moment. Much to your surprise, Mr. Arnaud walked into the customer courtesy lounge and extended his hand. After escorting you to the privacy of his office, he had informed you that your money was no good at his place of business. You protested mildly and offered to pay, but Mr. Arnaud would have none of it. As he walked you to your truck, he had assured you that he would write the work off. Although you had felt a little uncomfortable in accepting his generosity, you were more than just a little glad that you didn't have to take out a loan.

Now, it was payday of another kind. Apparently, Mr. Arnaud's son Tony had been found in possession of some stolen car-audio equipment. Mr. Arnaud had called to see if there was anything you could do to help with the situation. You know the arresting officer. He is an old friend who owes you a couple of favors, and you remind yourself that you have always liked to help salvageable kids stay out of the system. Still, you don't like being squeezed by Mr. Arnaud and aren't sure diverting Tony a second time will teach him the lesson that he needs to learn. And you also feel a little guilty that you had accepted that free transmission work.

Meanwhile, Mr. Arnaud is waiting for your call.

Questions for Discussion

1. How could accepting free auto repair compromise your professional and personal ethics?
2. Is Mr. Arnaud's son still salvageable?
3. How should you respond to the situation?

9

Double Bind

You have been working patrol with your partner, Ken, for more than three years, and you have never seen him this anxious when answering a domestic disturbance call.

"Ken, are you all right?" you ask.

"Yeah, I'll be OK. Probably some indigestion from eating that taco," Ken responds, popping another antacid in his mouth.

The last time you saw Ken this nervous was when his wife left him a year and a half ago. Because you are a woman, Ken had sought your advice then. Over countless cups of coffee, Ken had eventually confessed to you what you already had known—that the reason his wife left him was because he had run around on her one time too many.

For the last three months, Ken has seemed more settled and upbeat. He has indicated to you on several occasions that his new girlfriend has made "a new man" out of him. Whatever her effect, you have to agree that Ken has a more positive attitude about his work and his life. For that, you are grateful. The three of you even had lunch together last week.

As you and Ken approached the residence, you could hear shouting inside. You could also see the neighbors who had reported the disturbance peering out of their upstairs window.

After you announce yourselves as the police and knock loudly on the door several times, the noise inside calms down and a man, red-faced and obviously upset, opens the door. After you and Ken step inside the house, your jaw almost hits the floor. The wife with the tear-streaked face is none other than Ken's current girlfriend, Jane. When you turn to look at your partner, he averts his eyes. Not sure what to do, you decide to take Jane into an adjoining bedroom and ask Ken to talk with her husband in the living room. Jane is obviously embarrassed and continues to repeat over and over again, "I'm sorry." After you calm her down, you leave her sitting on the side of the bed and return to the living room, where you find her husband apologizing to a subdued Ken for upsetting the neighbors.

"I'm sorry for everything, officers. I just found out that my wife has been running around on me. We've been married for ten years and have a six-year-old son, who is over at his grandmother's. I got so angry when I found out that I lost my temper. If I could find the sorry bastard who's been trying to break up our family, you would probably have to arrest me for assault and battery!"

You and Ken ride in silence back to the precinct station. You volunteer to write up the report, and Ken nods in agreement as he quickly excuses himself.

Pulling the tab on a diet soft drink, you take a long drink from the can and reflect on your relationship with your partner and the report you are about to write.

Questions for Discussion

1. Should you discuss Ken's unethical behavior with him, or with your supervisor? Or should you simply ignore it?
2. How has Ken's behavior compromised his professional role as a police officer?

10

Convicted by DNA?

"Look, Mr. and Mrs. Johnson, your daughter was molested, and we need to get this scumbag back in prison."

Your partner, Lieutenant Ross Barton, a twenty-five-year veteran of the department, stood in the hallway of the hospital, pleading with the parents of a nine-year-old girl to help prosecute a known sex offender. Ross is a no-nonsense criminal investigator with a reputation for getting things done. You were assigned to him six months ago to learn the ropes of investigation. The Crimes Against Persons Unit was a detail you had aspired to be a part of since you joined the department three years ago. But this case, involving a little girl who was sexually molested by a convicted sex offender, was not one of the glory cases you had dreamed of handling. It was repulsive in nature, and it was difficult trying to communicate with the distraught parents. Although you could sympathize with the parents—after all, you have two young daughters of your own, one in kindergarten and the other in second grade—this didn't make your job any easier.

"Please, Lieutenant, look at it from our perspective. Our little girl is alive. Yes, she went through hell with this guy, but she's physically OK. We don't want to put her through the emotional trauma of having to testify against him. We just want to go home and start some sort of healing process," the girl's father had responded to Ross.

The little girl had been abducted while riding her bicycle in her neighborhood. The perpetrator, Steven Andrews, apparently enticed the girl into his house with the promise of some ice cream and an introduction to his fictitious nine-year-old daughter. The little girl was sexually molested but managed to run out of the house and report what happened to her parents, who notified police. The perpetrator, Andrews, was a registered sex offender who has engaged in this type of activity before. He is well known in the Crimes Against Persons Unit and had been watched carefully since his parole seven months ago.

After fruitlessly pleading with the parents, Ross walked down the hallway with you. "This guy's a dirtbag," he commented. "He did the same thing a couple of months ago to another little girl, and the parents didn't want to do anything about it, just like these jokers. Andrews digitally penetrates these kids so there's no semen. He's slick all right, but he's not getting away with it this time. That's it for him. He's going down!" Ross stated emphatically.

"But Ross, we have no physical evidence against this guy. The doctor and the forensic nurse both said there was evidence of penetration but no semen, neither on nor in the girl. Without that little girl's testimony we have no case," you argued.

"Oh yeah, we have a case. They didn't look at the clothing," Ross responded. "The nurse gave us the little girl's clothing in that bag, so I'll take it to forensics and see what they can find. I'll bet they'll find what we need. I know how these perps work. They ejaculate on the victim's clothing, not on or in their victim. If they find semen—Andrews's DNA—on those clothes of hers, we've got a case even without her testimony."

• • •

Seven months later, Ross looks back on the conviction of Steven Andrews. "Thank God for DNA," he says to you. "If it hadn't been for the forensics on this case, we would have never gotten this guy off the streets and back in prison where he belongs."

"I can't believe it either. What luck to find Andrews's semen on that little girl's clothing! Boy, you sure were right about him ejaculating on the clothes while he was digitally penetrating her," you respond.

Ross smiles and winks at you. "I'll let you in on a little trade secret, son. Always keep some physical evidence from perps like this from previous crimes. It may come in handy when you need evidence."

"What do you mean, Ross?" you ask.

"Well, two years ago this Andrews guy did the same thing to a little girl over in Taylorsville Community. We busted him, and the little girl who got molested had semen all over her. We collected it and froze it at the lab until we could match it up with Andrews. That was his first conviction here. Forensics had some of that clothing in evidence, and I procured some of it on this case and submitted it as the clothing of the little girl. Of course, the DNA matched Andrews's. So, justice has been served," Ross comments with a satisfied smirk on his face.

It is clear to you now what happened. Ross removed from the evidence room some old semen-covered garments from another case, and he submitted them to forensics as the little girl's clothing. He set Andrews up and got him convicted. At first, you are sickened by the idea that Ross would manufacture evidence against a defendant. But then you start to think about your own daughters and what you would have done if it had been one of them who were molested. Justice was served—wasn't it? And as a result, who knows how many little girls will now be protected from this monster? Still, as much as you try to justify Ross's actions, it leaves you with a sick feeling. What are you going to do?

Questions for Discussion

1. Is Ross a good cop or a bad cop? What were his intentions, and how do they conflict or agree with our justice system? What kind of person do you think he is morally?
2. Ross knew that Andrews was the perpetrator in this case. What does it matter that Ross manipulated the system to get a conviction? Did he not prevent other little girls from being molested or even killed by doing what he did?
3. Should Ross's partner report Ross's actions to superiors, or should he keep quiet? What would happen if he reported this to superiors? What would happen if he did not? What would you do—not *should* but *would*? Be honest in your answer.

11

"I've Got My Rights!"

Reverend Oliver of St. John's Community Church had called the station to report a heavily armed man standing in front of his church, shouting obscenities. Sergeant Tom Powell got the call, with two other cruisers on their way for back-up. Picking up his clipboard and shutting the cruiser's door behind him, Powell muttered to himself, "Doesn't look like this Sunday is going to be a day of rest."

He sized up the gaunt, elderly man standing on the front steps of the sanctuary, shouting at Reverend Oliver and several of his parishioners, whose church service he had interrupted. The protester looked to be in his seventies, sporting a long white beard, overalls, and a red flannel shirt. He carried a sign that read: "The Devil's Church Will Burn in Hell!" The man was packing a .45 caliber sidearm and had a deer rifle, complete with scope, strapped across his back. As Tom approached the man, he thought to himself, "I guess all the terrorists are not in the Middle East!"

The man stepped directly into Tom's path, shaking his sign, and shouted, "I know my rights, officer! Are you here to arrest these infernal blasphemers and sodomites, or a man of God?"

"What is your name, sir?" Tom replied calmly.

"Name's Willard Perkins—Elder Willard Perkins of The True Way Redeemer's Church."

Tom continued, "And what would be the purpose of your visit to St. John's?"

Willard Perkins's eyes blazed. "Officer, I'm here doing the Lord's work! Like the hymn says, I'm a Christian soldier in the army of the Lord, and He's done given me my marching orders! These blasphemers and sons of Satan married two homosexuals last week!"

Sergeant Powell glanced at the two backup cruisers that had arrived, then returned his gaze to the protestor. "I can see that you are concerned, Mr. Perkins, but I can also see that you are armed—"

"Armed with the sword of the Lord," Perkins interrupted. "Armed with the sword of the Lord!"

"That may be true, Mr. Perkins, but the reverend and his congregation feel threatened by your presence. Are your guns loaded?"

The old man looked incredulously at the sergeant. "Loaded? Hell yes, they're loaded! What kind of fool would go to do the Lord's work without his guns loaded? An unloaded weapon is no protection at all!"

Tom maintained his composure. "Still, you can understand why the reverend and his congregation might be concerned?"

Willard Perkins pursed his lips together and scowled. "They need to be concerned about judgment day and the hell that they will be burning in! It really don't matter what they think—or you, for that matter! I know my rights. Besides, I got myself a permit!"

"May I see it?"

"You sure can," Perkins replied as he fished a laminated card out of his shirt pocket.

As Tom checked the permit, Perkins narrowed his eyes suspiciously. "Officer, you need to be standing with me and God, instead of protecting these perverts!"

Willard Perkins's paperwork was in order. With his belligerence and aggressive demeanor, he walked a fine line between his protected right to bear arms and the safety and security of the members of St. John's. Reverend Oliver and his parishioners were peering out an open church window, observing Tom's interaction with the elderly protester. Several were taking pictures with their cell phones. Tom didn't want to escalate the situation, but he wasn't confident he would be able to talk Mr. Perkins into abandoning his post. At least, it was Sunday—fewer calls and more officers available for backup.

Questions for Discussion

1. How can Sergeant Powell respect the protester's rights and still maintain the confidence and security of the church members?
2. What potential risks and threats does this type of encounter pose, when prejudice, anger, and even hatred are evident in an armed protester?
3. Should Sergeant Powell attempt to escort Mr. Perkins away from the church, or should he remain at the church until the service is over and all the members and the reverend have left?

12

The Only Way?

Carrollsville is a city of approximately 165,000 situated in the Bible Belt of the southern United States. Although a major hub of four interstate highways, it has always maintained an easy lifestyle and a relatively low crime rate compared to similar cities in the South. Carrollsville boasts a state university campus with over 40,000 students, seven large industries, and a large lake for recreational boating and fishing. In recent years it has attracted a number of new retirees from various parts of the country. As a consequence, new subdivisions have been built over the past ten years, allowing the city to expand its boundaries through annexation.

The annexation efforts brought not only residential, manufacturing, and industrial areas into the city, but also a number of smaller businesses. Three of the newly annexed businesses are exotic dance bars and gentlemen's clubs. The three adult entertainment businesses are located separately, based on the nearness of interstate highways, and all three have been in business for over twenty years. Two of the clubs, the Bunny Tail and the Diamond Club, are in your patrol sector.

You are a police lieutenant in charge of seven patrol units in the northwestern area of the city. You have worked as an officer for the Carrollsville Police Department ever since you graduated college from twenty-seven years ago. You came up through the ranks as a patrolman, detective, patrol supervisory sergeant, and now a mid-level manager in patrol. You were born and raised in Carrollsville and never had any ambition to work anywhere else. Even as a high school student you were involved with the police department's Police Explorers Scout Program. It was then that you fell in love with the job of law enforcement. Now your only ambition is to retire, hopefully as a captain within the department, and devote the rest of your time to fishing in Lake Haven and playing with any grandkids that might come along.

"Bill, good to see you hard at work down here in the dungeon!"

You look up from your desk and are surprised to see both your captain and the deputy chief of police standing in your office doorway.

"What are you guys doing down here where all the work is done?" you jokingly respond.

"We've got a little situation we need some help with, Bill. The chief's behind it too, but I don't think he could find the elevator to come down here," Deputy Chief Mottern replies with a laugh.

"Well, it must be important for the both of you to come looking for me. What's up?"

"You know our new mayor campaigned on law and order and keeping the city clean and stuff," Captain Steadman states with a slight smirk. "Yeah, she's a real Queen Victoria when it comes to all this moral stuff."

Mottern chuckles and adds, "Well, she's hired this hot-shot lawyer from out of state to come in here and evaluate the adult business problem we have."

You look at both of them in puzzlement and ask, "What problem? There are only three adult businesses in the city: The Diamond Club, the Bunny Tail, and the Cocktail Lounge. I've never had any problems from the two in my sector. The Cocktail Lounge is in Lieutenant Rogers's sector and he's never had a problem either. We've never had any trouble to speak of from any of them since they were annexed into the city."

Mottern replies, "I know, and that's the 'situation' we need help with. The lawyer she hired has convinced the mayor that these three clubs are a magnet for criminal activity, prostitution, and drugs, and that their existence has increased the amount of sexually transmitted diseases in the city and lowered property values."

"She wants to motion the city council to create a new ordinance against these clubs and close them down," Captain Steadman adds.

"And she wants us to provide her with some documentation to support that position," Mottern adds, looking pointedly at you.

You stare at them both in disbelief and say, "Ed, Joe—we were all here when the city annexed those clubs. They've been here for over twenty years! They were never a problem for the county, and they haven't been a problem for us in the city. Hell, we have more problems from the sports bars and shopping center parking lots than we do from those clubs. I'm not defending their business, and I personally dislike those types of clubs. But this is a college town, and we've got more prostitution, drugs, STDs, and the like originating from fraternity houses than from these adult clubs! I know the managers of those clubs and they keep a pretty tight rein on the clientele. The clubs' signs are conservative and don't attract a lot of attention. And as for property values, didn't they just build a new subdivision next to the Bunny Tail four years ago? Those houses cost a lot more than what I live in! And that big church went up nearly across the street from the Diamond Club last year. We haven't heard any complaints from them. What does the mayor want us to do? We don't have any documentation to support her position!"

"Listen, Bill, you're preaching to the choir here. Joe and I both agree with you, and Lieutenant Rogers said the same thing about the Cocktail Lounge in his sector. The problem we have is that the mayor wants us to support HER position so she can run these businesses out. If we don't support her, she ain't going to support us, especially when it comes time for pay raises and budget approvals. Chief Ketron is between a rock and a hard place on this matter, and he wants us to do whatever we need to do to get documentation. He's behind us one hundred percent," Mottern replies.

"Behind us on what? What do you want me to do?" you ask, with a growing feeling of dread.

"We need documentation showing that these clubs are a police problem and have an adverse impact on the community. We need incident reports, arrest reports, even commentary on daily activity reports. All these things are computerized and can be easily edited, or new reports added into the system, reflecting a pattern over the past few years that shows these clubs are a nuisance and are hot spots for criminal activities, drug dealing, and so on," Captain Steadman answers.

You look incredulously at the two of them and respond in disgust, "In other words, you want me to generate false reports and manipulate records?"

Mottern shrugs and adds, "I know it doesn't sound good, but it's not like someone is getting set up to go to jail. It's just puttin' these people out of business—a dirty business. And it will guarantee the mayor's support for the department. We are facing some serious cutbacks in personnel and budgeting. But with the mayor's support, we'll be in pretty good shape the next few years. You know I'm retiring next year and Joe, here, a year after that. You have seniority as a lieutenant, and I can arrange for you to be promoted to deputy chief, and Lieutenant Rogers can get the captain slot after Joe retires. We've already spoken to Rogers, and he's on board with this. He was reluctant, too, but he knows the score. Look, take a day to think about it and I'll holler at you tomorrow. I'm sure you'll see it's the only way."

As Mottern and Steadman leave your office, Mottern's words keep echoing in your head, "It's the only way . . . it's the only way . . . it's the only way."

Questions for Discussion

1. What are Lieutenant Bill Crowder's options? Is Deputy Chief Mottern's way the "only way" in this situation?
2. If word got out that records had been manufactured against the adult businesses, who do you think would be blamed? Who would Chief Ketron, Deputy Chief Mottern, and Captain Steadman point the figure at?
3. If you did manufacture false reports, an ordinance was offered in city council, and the adult business establishments subsequently sued the city, what would you say about the impact of the adult businesses in the city on the witness stand, under oath?

13

The War at Home

Neal Cronkhite popped another stick of gum in his mouth while looking at the man standing on the porch who is talking to his partner, Ralph. Stepping inside the house, Neal could see Sally Davis in the bedroom, packing a suitcase for herself and her two-year-old daughter, Ginny. Sally's father was on his way to pick the two of them up. Her husband, Paul, the man on the porch, had recently returned from his third tour in Afghanistan. As Sally closed the suitcase, she motioned to Neal. Closing the front door behind him, Neal walked into the bedroom, where Sally was zipping up her young daughter's parka.

"Officer Cronkhite, I'm worried about Paul—about what he might do when Ginny and I leave with my father," Sally said nervously, looking over her shoulder to see whether Paul was within earshot.

Handing her his card, Neal offered Sally the most reassuring gesture he could muster. "Don't worry about your husband. If he threatens you or your father in any way, call me at this number."

"I'm not worried about what he might do to us. I'm worried what he might do to himself! He has come home from each tour more depressed and despondent than before. At least he used to have his job to look forward to, but when he told his boss about being called up for this last tour, he was told that the company would have to hire another driver. I'm working two jobs just to keep our heads above water. I'm afraid my husband is at the end of his rope."

Neal looked at the bruise on the side of Sally's head and the redness still apparent on the nape of her neck. He shook his head and said, "I know it's a hard time for you, Mrs. Davis, and that you don't want your husband arrested, but you and I both know that bruise and the redness around your neck didn't happen because you slipped on the stairs."

Continuing to look over her shoulder, Sally whispered, "I took him to the veteran's hospital at Mountain Home to get some help, but he stopped going two weeks ago. When he stopped going, he started back drinking again. I called the counselor there today—here's his number—but he hasn't got back to me yet. If they could just get Paul some help . . ."

Sally looked as if she were about to cry. Neal hated it when women cried. He watched her as she picked up her daughter and thought to himself, "What a mess!" Before he had time to try to think things through, Ralph opened the front door and said, "Her father's here."

"Look, Mrs. Davis, after you leave with your father, I'll talk some more with your husband and my partner and see what we can come up with. I'm not making any promises . . ."

"Thank you, Officer Cronkhite, thank you so much."

Scribbling a number on the back of a paper napkin, Sally thrust it at Neal. "Will you call me when you know something?"

"I'll call you," said Neal in his most reassuring tone of voice.

Neal and Ralph leaned against their cruiser while Paul Davis sat in the back seat.

"Hell, Neal, veteran or no veteran, there's no question that Davis was beating on his wife. Our shift's done in an hour. I say let's book him and let the jail staff and DA's office figure it out."

Neal stared down at his shoes. "His wife gave me his counselor's number. If I could get in touch with him, he might be able to admit him to Mountain Home."

"You can do what you want to, Partner, but I got a hot date tonight so if you don't want to go by the book, you're on your own," Ralph replied with a grin.

Neal sighed and muttered, as much to himself as to his partner, "Unfortunately, life doesn't tend to go by the book."

Questions for Discussion

1. Domestic situations are often messy and complicated and can prove to be difficult challenges for responding police officers. Neal's partner doesn't want to go the extra mile, suggesting that instead they just go "by the book." Does he have a point? Is there any guarantee that the counselor will get Paul admitted to Mountain Home or that Paul will even agree to go?
2. Should Neal make the extra attempt to try to help Paul, a veteran whose domestic violence is, at least in part, influenced by PTSD?
3. What is the officers' responsibility if they allow Paul to stay home by himself after his wife and daughter have left? Would they be legally liable if Paul harmed himself?

Section II

ETHICS AND THE COURTS

The criminal and appellate courts are, in a sense, the center of the criminal justice system around which all the other components revolve. Everything that police do and everything that correctional professionals do is, to some extent, influenced by the decisions of those in the court system. Police procedures are governed by court decisions regarding arrests, search and seizure, interpretation of statutes, and case decisions. Those in the correctional system are also affected by case decisions regarding sentencing procedures, community alternatives, the civil rights of prisoners, and what should and/or can be done in the name of treatment.

We have a sense that the "rule of law" is static and formulistic; that is, the same answers can always be found by applying legal principles. This is not always true. Further, there is a difference between law and ethics. The "legal" answer may not be, in everyone's opinion, the "ethical" answer to a situation. For instance, when the Supreme Court defines "the law of the land"; unless or until the decision is overturned, it is the law, even though in many decisions (such as abortion, eminent domain, campaign financing, and First Amendment cases) many people vehemently disagree with the decision. Observers note that who is appointed to the Supreme Court has a great deal of influence over the decisions in controversial areas of the law. The conservative Justices (Chief Justice Roberts and Justice Alito) have recently been joined by so-called liberal justices (Justices Sotomayor and Kagan). As with all decisions on the bench, the law is less (or more) than a collection of formulaic rules and involves a great deal of interpretation. The legal definition of any action does not always resolve the issue, and some decisions continue to be moral and ethical dilemmas for individuals.

Ethical issues often arise in relation to the duties of one's profession. Each actor in the criminal court has a role to play. Prosecutors are supposed to pursue justice, but in most cases this means trying to convince the jury of the guilt of the accused. Defense attorneys attempt to show either that the defendant is actually innocent of the charges or that there are mitigating circumstances that lessen the defendant's guilt. The judge is akin to a referee, making decisions on motions and testimony. Judges are supposed to remain unbiased, but many judges lean toward the defense or the prosecution. In those states that elect judges, they are very sensitive to public opinion even though they are supposed to apply justice "blindly." Jury members are supposed to abide by strict rules that govern how they are to make a decision regarding guilt or innocence and the sentence to be imposed. Other court personnel are involved to a greater or lesser extent in the process, and they all have duties to perform and opportunities to engage in ethical or unethical behaviors.

A basic concept of the American criminal justice system is due process. The Fifth and Fourteenth Amendments of the Constitution provide for due process rights for all individuals faced with deprivations of life, liberty, or property by government officials. As discussed in the last section, often these due process rights of offenders are perceived as barriers to "justice," especially when there is a strong belief in the guilt of the offender, and the due process right is perceived as a "technicality." However, recent exonerations of death-row inmates should instruct all of us in the danger of subverting due process. How could innocent people be convicted and sentenced to death row? Usually it can be traced to individuals in the criminal justice process who attempt to manipulate the system to achieve what they feel is a desired end—the conviction of the accused. A more subtle, insidious problem arises when actors in the system do not take their role seriously. If, for instance, defense attorneys begin to believe that everyone is guilty and feel that putting much energy into cases is futile, then the system fails. When prosecutors believe that due process is a game with winners and losers, they lose sight of justice. Finally, when judges let their personal biases cloud their decision-making abilities, then the system becomes "the rule of man," subject to all the vagaries, foibles and weaknesses of humans, rather than the rule of law.

Judges

The judge has two very distinct areas of power. The first is in the ability to rule on motions presented by either the prosecutor or the defense attorney. These decisions shape the course of the trial and, to a large degree, help to determine whether an individual will be found guilty. Whether a piece of evidence is admitted, whether a witness is allowed on the stand, whether certain testimony can be presented, whether a jury member is excused for cause, whether an attorney receives the continuance he asks for, whether a motion to dismiss is granted—these are all decisions made by the judge on the bench. The "rule of law" should be guiding such decisions, but, in reality, the decision making is much more subjective than most people think. Of course, judges' decisions may be reversed on appeal, but this is statistically unlikely. More subtly, the judge's demeanor and behavior can influence the jury. If he or she shows a clear bias toward or against one of the attorneys, the jury picks up on this bias and may be influenced. To a large extent, the judge is the most powerful individual in the courtroom.

The second major area of power that rests with the judge is the power to sentence. Most of the time, judges—not juries—make sentencing decisions. Although many jurisdictions now have sentencing guidelines and various forms of mandatory sentence structures that take the sentencing decisions away from judges, judges in many states still have a great deal of discretion in their sentencing decisions. How does one decide what sentence a defendant "deserves?" Do personal biases influence this decision? What factors should influence the decision? Judges may choose from a broad range of judicial alternatives, particularly when the offender is nonviolent. The presentence report, prepared by the probation office in most jurisdictions, offers background information on the offender, and victim and/or witness statements are now routinely incorporated into the record as well. The concept of "justice" is fairly amorphous, however, and different judges often come up with widely disparate sentences. Thus, fairness may always be in the eye of the beholder, but judges always have the ethical duty to make such decisions fairly, without personal bias or favoritism affecting their decision.

Prosecutors

It has been said that the decision whether or not to prosecute is one of the least studied decision points in the system, and the prosecutor's office one of the least studied areas of the criminal justice system. Many people do not realize the extent of discretion that prosecutors have in whether to charge and what to charge in criminal cases. Although police officers make arrests, in some jurisdictions prosecutors must approve the charge. In all jurisdictions prosecutors may dismiss, reduce, or increase the charges against criminal defendants. Although some jurisdictions use grand juries to obtain indictments, the majority of charges are based on "informations" filed by the prosecutor's office, not indictments (which come from a grand jury). How do prosecutors decide whether or not to charge? In most cases, the sufficiency of the evidence is the most important consideration.

After charging, the next point of discretion is the plea bargain. Prosecutors have and use the power to reduce charges in return for guilty pleas. Plea bargaining has been called a "necessary evil" in the criminal justice system. It is obvious that without it the system would see more cases going to trial, and that would increase the costs of the system tremendously. On the other hand, critics on both sides of the conservative and liberal continuum argue that it is contradictory to the pursuit of justice. Conservatives argue that offenders should be charged with what they did, not some lesser charge; liberals argue that prosecutors "pad" charges with accusations they know they could not prove in court in order to have something to bargain with. In reality, some descriptions indicate that both prosecutors and defense attorneys share roughly similar ideas of what each crime "deserves" by way of punishment, and the general nature of the process is one of an assembly line rather than a contest between dueling opponents.

Defense Attorneys

Defense attorneys are the guardians of due process. Even if their client is guilty, they have a duty to ensure that the state (or federal government) has followed the proper procedure leading up to the arrest and during the trial of the defendant. Because of their clientele, the legal community and society at large may look down upon criminal defense attorneys. On the other hand, one could argue that no other job is more important, since the defense attorney stands as a buffer between the individual and the awesome power of the state. It might be argued that without defense attorneys there would be more innocent people in prisons and on death row.

Ethical issues for defense attorneys generally fall under the categories of either working too zealously for the defendant (and violating rules and/or laws in doing so), or, more often, not working hard enough for the client, letting burnout and lethargy compromise their performance. Defense attorneys who are either legal aid attorneys or attorneys who take court appointments generally have very large caseloads, and it is easy to see why they may let some cases slide through without due diligence in their defense. It should always be remembered, however, that in the end the system only works when everyone involved understands and performs his or her duties. In the criminal justice system, the law dictates what should happen but it is the people working in the system who create the reality of justice.

Suggestions for Further Reading

Aronson, R., & McMurtrie, J. (2007). The use and misuse of high-tech evidence by prosecutors: Ethical and evidentiary issues. *Fordham Law Review, 76*, 1453–1538.

Court, J. N. (2000). *The lawyers' book of ethics*. Kansas City, MO: Andrews McMeel.

Cunningham, L. (1999). Taking on testilying: The prosecutor's response to in-court police deception. *Criminal Justice Ethics, 18*(1), 26–40.

Fitzgerald, P. (2009). Thoughts on the ethical culture of a prosecutor's office. *Washington Law Review, 84*, 11–35.

Fountain, H. (2009, May 12). Plugging holes in the science of forensics. Retrieved from http://www.nytimes.com/2009/05/12/science/12fore.html

Giannelli, P., & McMunigal, K. (2007). Prosecutors, ethics, and expert witnesses. *Fordham Law Review, 76*(3), 1493–1537.

Hashimoto, E. (2008). Toward ethical plea bargaining. *Cardozo Law Review, 30,* 949–963.

Kaufman, K. (2003). *Legal ethics* (the West legal studies series). Clifton Park, NY: Thomson Delmar Learning.

Kirchmeier, J., Greenwald, S., Reynolds, H., & Sussman, J. (2009). Vigilante justice: Prosecutor misconduct in capital cases. *The Wayne Law Review, 55,* 1327–1385.

Kreiger, M. (2009). A twenty-first century ethos for the legal profession: Why bother? *Denver University Law Review, 86,* 865–900.

Medwed, D. (2009). The prosecutor as minister of justice: Preaching to the unconverted from the post-conviction pulpit. *Washington Law Review, 84,* 35–66.

Meekins, T. (2007). Risky business: Criminal specialty courts and the ethical obligations of the zealous criminal defender. *Berkeley Journal of Criminal Law, 12,* 75–135.

Pollock, J. (2011). *Ethics in crime and justice: Dilemmas and decisions* (7th ed.). Belmont, CA: Wadsworth.

Radelet, M., Bedau, H., & Putnam, C. (1992). *In spite of innocence.* Boston: Northeastern University Press.

Rhode, D. (2000). *In the interests of justice: Reforming the legal profession.* New York: Oxford University Press.

Shaffer, T., & Cochran, R. (2007). "Technical" defenses: Ethics, morals, and the lawyer as friend. *Clinical Law Review, 14,* 337–353.

Swisher, K. (2009). The judicial ethics of criminal law adjudication. *Arizona State Law Journal, 41,* 755–828.

Wendel, W. B. (2006). Ethical lawyering in a morally dangerous world. *The Georgetown Journal of Legal Ethics, 1*(19).

Zacharias, F., & Green, B. (2009). The duty to avoid wrongful convictions: A thought experiment in the regulation of prosecutors. *Boston University Law Review, 89,* 1–59.

Zitrin, R., & Langford, C. (1999). *The moral compass of the American lawyer.* New York: Ballantine.

1

Diversion or Subversion?

You pore over the pre-sentence evaluation. Two intoxicated college females, one DUI and the other trying to run from police officers. Both have no prior arrests, and both are nursing majors at the local college. As judge, you must decide whether to sentence them to probation or place them in a diversion program. Further complicating your options, you have to choose between a private probation agency (Accelerated Diversion, Inc.) and the state's probation diversion program. The private agency appears to be very progressive and boasts an impressive array of alcohol and drug education, counseling, and follow-up services, while the state agency's services seem to be more traditional and limited. In addition, the attorney representing the two students has indicated they would prefer to be referred to Accelerated Diversion, Inc.

You have been a judge for ten years, and you take your job seriously. It would be easy to accede to the young women's wishes, yet you find yourself becoming increasingly uneasy about what you are hearing through the grapevine about Accelerated Diversion. At worst, the rumors suggest that Accelerated Diversion is nothing more than a fee collection agency, where the fees they collect determine salaries. Accelerated Diversion's critics contend that probation officers spend very little time with their clients and what appears impressive on paper is, for the most part, nonexistent in practice. You do know for a fact that the executive director of Accelerated Diversion makes $100,000 a year, which is considerably more than what other comparable agency directors make in your city. Still, clients, for the most part middle class, seem pleased with their services.

In addition, the state department of probation has a fairly limited approach to alcohol and drug diversion, and they do not appear to be very interested in any new or creative approaches. Still, you have known the people who have worked there for a long time. They are solid and dedicated, if overworked, corrections professionals. What would be best for the two young women? Which agency would have the greatest impact on them?

QUESTIONS FOR DISCUSSION

1. Do you, as the judge, have any other options you can think of? Should you allow your personal beliefs about the private agency to interfere with your sentence?
2. How should private agencies be controlled and/or monitored to insure they are providing the services they should?
3. What are ethical criteria for sentencing decisions? What are unethical criteria?
4. Can justice be "bought" in our criminal justice system?
5. Do judges, other criminal justice professionals, and the system in general have a moral obligation to ensure that private corrections agencies provide meaningful and effective correctional services? What are some ways in which such agencies could be monitored and evaluated in order to make them more accountable?

2

Juvenile Probation

Boot Camp or Boot Hill?

"Your honor, I know I've done wrong . . . more than once . . . but I know I can do right, if you will just give me one more chance with Ms. Simpson, my probation officer. I couldn't take boot camp. My nerves wouldn't stand it. Just ask my mother."

Alex's mother quickly added, "Dr. Platt, our family psychiatrist, has indicated in Alex's file that he couldn't withstand the rigors of such an experience." Getting teary-eyed, she continued, "You will also note in the report that Alex's brother, Louis, committed suicide while at boot camp in the Marines. We thought the experience would straighten him out, but it was a terrible mistake. His death has put us all through a terrible ordeal and has made a lasting impression on Alex."

"That's right, Judge Arnett," said Alex, "I've never been the same since my brother died."

Scanning Alex's social history, you locate the psychiatrist's report and find that Alex's mother's responses are essentially accurate. You also note that Ms. Simpson's comments suggest that Alex is highly manipulative, especially concerning his mother's and father's feelings of guilt regarding his brother's death. In addition, you note that this is the seventeen-year-old's third and most serious offense, breaking and entering.

You are considering two basic sentencing options. You could sentence Alex to two years at the juvenile training school or give him the option of attending the 90-day juvenile boot camp. You could also extend his traditional probation sentence.

It seems evident to you that Alex has benefited little from psychiatric counseling. In fact, his parents probably need such services more than he does. It is equally apparent to you that Alex isn't a particularly stable individual and probably is, to some extent, affected by his brother's death.

There is another option, but one that is much more expensive. An Outward Bound program is operating near the national forest that has one staff member for every five students. Its success rate has been as impressive as its price tag. Boot camp is politically popular, but you are not very impressed with the long-term results. Within six months of their graduation from boot camp, you have seen many of the same young men standing before you in court with new offenses. Finally, you know in your "heart of hearts" that Alex would not last long physically or emotionally in the juvenile training school.

It is time to render your decision. You must balance what is in Alex's best interest with the needs of the community. Is Outward Bound really worth the expense? Boot camp has helped a lot of young men, but is it for everyone? More importantly, is it for Alex?

Questions for Discussion

1. As a judge, you are in a moral quandary. Alex needs structure and discipline; boot camp can give him that. Alex is also unstable. Would boot camp be too damaging to him psychologically?
2. Are there other alternatives that you can identify that will help Alex and/or reduce the costs associated with the Outward Bound program? What is the right thing to do?
3. What is a judge's duty? Is his or her primary duty to society or to the victim? Would the victim of Alex's B & E care that his brother died? *Should* the victim care?
4. Is it unethical to let cost be a primary consideration in determining the most effective program for Alex?

3

The Court and Child Abuse

As a lawyer, you have enjoyed private practice. However, after ten years of successful practice, you have decided to enter public service and politics. You and your family realized that public service does not have the financial rewards of a private practice, but your ten-year law practice solidified your financial situation. Over the years you made some important personal connections and a good name for yourself. On your first attempt at public service, you were elected county prosecutor. Being a prosecutor was a different kind of law practice; your new job was to convict people in the name of the state instead of defending them.

Of the variety of cases you prosecuted, some naturally stirred your passion more than others. Because you were a family man, the crime of child abuse was one of the crimes that always seemed to make you press harder. You always attempted to prosecute abusive parents to the full extent of the law and have their children removed to a nonthreatening environment. Trials for this offense always proved to be an emotional experience for you.

Your career as county prosecutor progressed rapidly. Eventually you were appointed a family court judge, a position that, again, proved to be a different world. You now have to evaluate facts objectively, rather than approach the case primarily from a prosecutor's or defense lawyer's point of view.

Your first case of child abuse as judge proves to be a very difficult experience. The family is very prominent in the community. Both husband and wife are successful professionals, highly regarded by their colleagues. The police discovered the abuse as a result of a family disturbance call. The abuse had apparently been taking place for a short time and, because of the family's community standing, it had been covered up. The abuse seemed to have resulted from marital problems that had led both parents to heavy drinking. During an argument between the couple, their seven-year-old son interrupted them. From then on they focused and projected their problems onto the child. The actual physical abuse was usually a belt strap across the back of the young boy. The psychological damage to the youth as a result of his parents' behavior was, of course, impossible to measure. You are also troubled by another subtle aspect of this particular case. Apparently, the child in question spends most of the time when he is not in school with a variety of sitters, typically seeing his parents for one or two hours each night. He also frequently spends his weekends with grandparents.

You are not the county prosecutor or defense attorney now. You are the judge and you must try to do what is best for all concerned, especially the boy. Should you take him out of his home or not? If you do, you will be taking him away from the place where he lives and from his natural parents. His parents are in the financial position to do a great deal for their son, whereas a government agency could not. More important, the boy does love his parents and seems to want to stay with them. On the other hand, if you do not remove him from the home, he could be subjected to even more severe abuse. The court experience might open the eyes of the parents to their need for professional help in solving their problems and child-abuse tendencies, but there is no way to be sure.

Questions for Discussion

1. What decision should you make regarding this case? What should guide your decision making? What is in the best interest of the child and the parents?
2. What specific recommendations should you make regarding the family's treatment program?
3. In a situation like this, how does one prioritize punishment and treatment? Should the parents be punished for abusing their child or helped with the goal of their not doing it anymore?
4. What should a judge do when he or she is confused or unsure about how to resolve a case?

4

Child Rapist

You are an assistant district attorney in a small circuit court region. The region consists of three counties with an average population of 80,000 people per county. The community you serve is primarily composed of middle-class people with middle-class values. Having come from a large city, you are particularly impressed with the small-town atmosphere and easy way of life.

The district attorney general hired you straight out of law school two years ago. You felt that a job with the DA's office would be an excellent opportunity to gain needed experience and develop a reputation as a good lawyer. Your ambition is to enter the political arena and perhaps run for state representative in a couple of years. You have stressed a "law and order" image in order to accomplish your career ambitions.

As you prepare to look over the court docket for tomorrow's cases, your secretary advises you that Sheriff's Investigator John Wainwright is waiting to see you.

"John, come in. I was going to call you about our burglary case tomorrow. You didn't have to come over here in person today."

"Thanks, Dave, but I need to talk with you about another matter. You know, we arrested a young man by the name of Fred Granger a couple of days ago for rape, and I wanted to fill you in on some details," the investigator begins.

"Yes, I was at the arraignment, remember?" you respond jokingly.

Fred Granger is a twenty-two-year-old white male who works in a nearby factory. He has a high school education and has no prior felony arrests or convictions, but he does have a previous conviction for DUI two years ago and one for possession of marijuana three years ago. He has been charged with the rape of a 13-year-old girl under state code 3712702:

> Any adult who carnally knows a child under the age of fourteen by sexual intercourse shall be guilty of the capital offense of rape. The punishment for same shall be not less than ten years nor more than thirty years in the state penitentiary without parole. It shall be no defense that the child consented to the act or that the defendant was ignorant of the age of the child.

The punishment for this offense is no different than for the crime of forcible rape in your state. Fred Granger was arrested on a complaint from the parents of a thirteen-year-old girl named Debbie. It seems Fred picked Debbie up for a date, went to the lake, and had sexual intercourse with her. It was a clear violation of the law and an apparently easy conviction, since Fred admitted to arresting officers that he had sex with Debbie.

"So, what information do you have for me, John?" you ask.

"We've obtained statements from everyone involved. This is basically what went down. Fred knew Debbie's sister, Nina, who is twenty years old. Fred and Nina had gone out before on a couple of dates in the past and have had intercourse. It seems Nina and her younger sister, Debbie, have the reputation of being 'easy.' Anyway, Fred called Nina for a date and Nina wasn't at home. Debbie answered the phone and started flirting with Fred. Fred asked Debbie if she wanted to go with him to the lake and Debbie agreed. Debbie apparently wore a very revealing bathing suit and 'came on' to Fred. They had intercourse and Fred dropped Debbie back home. Debbie's parents inquired about her activities for the day and Debbie told them everything, even about the sex. That's when we got the call. Fred states that he thought Debbie was over eighteen and that Debbie consented to having sex with him. Debbie supports this story. Both of them were drinking beer at the lake," said the investigator.

"Yes, well, I see. But, it's no defense for Fred to be ignorant of her actual age and no defense for him that Debbie consented. He probably got her drunk anyway. The law is clear on this matter," you advise.

"Yes, I know. But this Debbie has a reputation of being very promiscuous. She is very open about the fact that she consented. She now says she's in love with Fred. Needless to say, her parents aren't very happy about her attitude, but they seem to have very little control over her or her sister. Besides, anyone who's seen Debbie could make a mistake about her age." The investigator pulls out and shows you a recent photograph of Debbie.

The photograph surprises you. You had never seen the victim, but from the photograph Debbie looks well over twenty years old.

"Hey, she does look at least twenty," you respond. "She certainly would have fooled me."

"Yeah. Anyone might assume that," the investigator replies.

Looking over the statements that the investigator brought, you begin to feel uneasy about the case. In a legal sense, Fred is a criminal. He violated the state law. He has no legal defense. The girl is under fourteen, which means she cannot testify that she consented. The fact that she has had intercourse before also cannot be used as a defense for Fred. It seems to be an open-and-shut case. Fred is looking at ten to thirty years with no chance of parole. Even if he got the minimum ten years, it is still a stiff punishment for ignorance. You decide to call on the district attorney general for advice.

"Yes, Dave. I see why you are concerned. It seems to me you have three options here. One, you could *nolle prosequi* the case (a formal entry on the record by the prosecuting attorney that he will not prosecute the case further). Two, you could reduce charges through a plea-bargain arrangement. Or, three, you could prosecute to the fullest extent of the law. It's basically a choice between legal ethics and personal ethics. Legal ethics would dictate that you prosecute to the fullest. A crime has been committed and you are sworn to uphold the law. In that sense, it would not be legally ethical for you to *nolle prosequi* or plea bargain when you have such a strong case. And, if you did, it might affect your political career. The news media and the public would not take your letting a 'child rapist' off without comment. On the other hand, your personal ethics dictate that this Fred fellow is not a typical criminal. He's guilty of stupidity maybe. But, apparently when you look at Debbie, you can see why. If you prosecuted the case, the jury might see Debbie the way Fred saw her and acquit him, but that is a big chance to take. Juries are unpredictable, and you can't bring up the fact that she 'looks' of age. I don't know, Dave. It's your decision. I'll back you on whatever you decide."

Questions for Discussion

1. Statutory rape can present one of the most challenging ethical dilemmas to a district attorney. How would the community and justice be served by prosecuting this case? How could the correctional system "rehabilitate" Fred or, for that matter, help Debbie?
2. What do you think would happen with Fred if he were found guilty and received ten years without chance of parole? Would such a sentence be, in a sense, immoral—in terms of justice served?
3. What is the prosecutor's duty?
4. What is the ethical action to take? Why?

5

A Question of Credibility

"What is it now?" you snap to the office secretary, who has buzzed you for the tenth time in 10 minutes. You have been trying to get an answer ready for a motion to exclude evidence, and it must be filed by 5:00 PM today. It is now 3:30 PM, and you still have a lot of work to do before you can get it to the county clerk's office.

"There is a person out here who wants to talk to you about a case," Sandra, your secretary, has poked her head in your office door and rolls her eyes to indicate that you probably *don't* want to talk to the person who wants to talk to you.

"Which case?" It's automatic—you can't help yourself, you always want to learn all the facts before making a decision.

"It's the drug case . . . Ramirez, Romero . . . something like that."

At this point a well-dressed young woman has come up behind Sandra and interrupts.

"It is Ramiro. He is my brother, and he is innocent."

"Ma'am, I really can't talk about the case. It's not appropriate for me to . . ."

But the woman has already managed to sidestep Sandra into your office and has boldly taken the seat meant for visitors. You wearily wave your secretary away and explain to her that it is not appropriate for prosecutors to discuss a case without the defense attorney present. Despite your protestations, she insists that she has important information about the case and needs to be heard because the defense attorney would not listen to her.

Christine Ramiro speaks rapidly and to the point. It is obvious that she is intelligent and educated. Basically her story is that the undercover officer who identified her brother as the individual who sold him drugs was well-known in the neighborhood, and no one would have been stupid enough to sell drugs to him. In addition, she knows that the day her brother was supposed to have sold drugs to the accuser, he was at work—and her brother's boss was willing to testify to that fact. Finally, she passionately argues that the officer, who wasn't even a "real" police officer but rather a temporary hire with federal anti-drug monies, had made accusations against many people in her neighborhood, half of whom had been arrested, and she knows for a fact that most of them had nothing to do with the drug trade.

You explain to her that what she said could be used by the defense attorney, but she replies that the defense attorney, appointed by the state, is only interested in getting her brother to plead to a possession charge that would still be a felony conviction.

After telling her you will look into it, you make a quick call to a lieutenant you know in the police department. Without going into too much detail about why you want to know, you ask him about the agent who is the major witness in the Ramiro case as well as a dozen other drug cases. He seems suspicious and guarded in his responses, enough to indicate to you that the cases may be shaky. On the other hand, if you have an officer of the law willing to testify that he made a buy from the accused, it is up to the jury to determine the credibility of the officer compared to the defendant. To make matters even more complicated, it is now 4:30, and you still haven't finished the task at hand.

Questions for Discussion

1. Does the prosecutor have a duty to look "beyond the evidence" in a case like this? How much time and energy should prosecutors devote to looking for innocence when they are presented with evidence of guilt by law enforcement?
2. Would it make a difference if the information came from someone who wasn't clearly "intelligent and educated"?
3. Some may recognize some of the facts of this case as being close to what happened in Tulia, Texas, when an undercover officer's testimony was instrumental in convicting a large percentage of the black population in this small town. Only after those accused were convicted and some served prison time was it reported that he had lied and was eventually convicted of perjury himself. What could have been done to prevent this from happening?

6

It's a Rat Race, and the Best Rat Wins

You have been a prosecutor for less than a year. Most of the other prosecutors in the office are generous with their advice, and you have learned a lot in the year since you graduated from law school. One of the senior prosecutors—Bruce Ralston—is a jokester around the office but is considered one of the best litigators in the office. He is funny, fearless, and the source of some outrageous office pranks. For instance, one night he nailed the door shut to another DA's office so when the poor guy came in the next morning, he unlocked the door and pulled and pulled on it, without success, much to the amusement of everyone watching. He had to call maintenance to get the nails removed, which made him late for court, and the judge threatened him with contempt because his excuse sounded so implausible. Although Bruce denied it, it was fairly common knowledge that he was the culprit.

He was equally unpredictable in his trial tactics. Others have told you that Bruce would "push the envelope" to get evidence in or to get a jury to buy into his theory of the case. One time he re-enacted the crime by having the medical examiner-witness show how the victim was decapitated, using the courtroom dummy. The head flew across the room and rolled right in front of the jury. Needless to say the defense attorney was extremely perturbed by the demonstration. Another time, he offered a confused defendant a "double or nothing" deal. He asked the defendant if he wanted to gamble—if the verdict came back guilty he'd get twice the time as what was being offered now. The defendant was seriously contemplating the wager until his attorney told him that the prosecutor couldn't bet on sentencing.

Today, you watched him in trial. He was by turns condescending, intimidating, and sympathetic, depending on the witness. In the closing he argued passionately that "if the victim's blood is on his clothing, it is because the defendant put it there," waving a dirty, torn t-shirt stained with blood, for emphasis. The victim was a homeless man who was found stabbed to death. The defendant was another homeless man who was found with the victim's possessions. It looked like a slam-dunk case, especially with the jury gazing in rapt attention as the bloody t-shirt was waved in front of them. You could see their eyes going back and forth, following the gruesome display.

Later, you are talking with Bruce back in his office about the case, and looking through the file. It appears there is not much direct evidence to link the defendant to the killing. There were no witnesses and the victim's blood was not found on him. You wonder how that could be.

"If the victim bled so much, you'd think some of it would have ended up on the defendant," you muse to yourself as you scan the documents in the file.

"The victim didn't bleed much at all, the doc says. It was a deep puncture in the back and he bled out into the ground," Bruce answered you, even though you hadn't directly asked the question.

"Well, how'd the blood get on the front . . ." at this point you stopped talking because you were reading a blood analysis report from the crime lab that appeared to say that the blood found on the t-shirt was not the victim's. In fact, it wasn't even human blood. You look up at Bruce, who has an expression of smugness mixed with a little guilt and with a look that says, "So what?"

He explains that the t-shirt was found in the victim's possession but that he wasn't wearing it when he was found. It appeared likely that the blood was from his dog that had been hit by a car earlier in the day.

"But you told the jury the blood was the victim's!" You are shocked that he would lie to the jury like that.

"No I didn't," he explained. "I said that *if* there was the victim's blood on the t-shirt, it was because the defendant did it. I didn't say there *was* the victim's blood there, did I? Hey, it's a rat race, you know—you gotta do what you need to do to hit the finish line. Don't you think that the other side does the same sort of stuff?"

You know that he has misled the jury and violated the spirit, if not the letter, of the law. On the other hand, it was not a crucial piece of evidence. The presence or absence of blood on the t-shirt was not exculpatory or inculpatory evidence. At most, it created an emotional response in the jury that might have affected their decision making. Still, you wondered if the judge knew that the t-shirt did not have the defendant's blood on it, since the evidence brought out in trial simply established that the t-shirt was the defendant's. You know that the defense attorney is a young kid, fresh out of law school, who is even more naïve than you. You wonder what, if anything, you should do about Bruce's little stunt.

Questions for Discussion

1. Where is the line between "zealous prosecution" and a subversion of the due process system?

2. Do you think there is an ethical duty to inform the judge of what you know? What about the defense attorney?
3. Do you think that the state bar would sanction Bruce for such behavior?

7

Everyone Does It

You have enjoyed your summer internship in a defense attorney's law office. During the last month you have been allowed to sit at the defense table and help prepare notes for Thomas Deffens, the attorney. You have also been able to sit in on interviews with clients and witnesses, read police reports, and go out with Mr. Deffens to evaluate evidence in the police evidence room. You have really enjoyed the work and you admire Mr. Deffens, who seems to be an excellent attorney.

Today you are with him in the courthouse. You have discovered that many attorneys spend every morning in the courthouse whether or not they have cases pending because after docket call, the judges assign the indigent cases. Mr. Deffens, like most of the other attorneys in town, take court appointments in addition to private clients. In fact, you think probably about three-fourths of the clientele are court appointed.

"Sugar, you are looking especially sweet today!"

Deffens leaned over Julie Conners's desk and flirted outrageously. Julie was Judge Anderson's court administrator, and you knew that one of the reasons Deffens got so many cases was because she liked him. Although he was friendly and somewhat flirtatious with all women, the court administrators were the recipients of intense flattery and you knew it was not a coincidence. Although cases were supposed to be rotated among all attorneys on "the list," you knew that Deffens received more than his fair share.

"I believe you will break my heart if you don't leave that husband of yours and fly off with me to Tahiti."

Julie Conners giggled, and you groaned inwardly. It was so lame you wouldn't think they would fall for it, but they did.

Later that day you headed back to court to file some papers and Deffens asked you to stop by Judge Anderson's court and give an envelope to Julie. As you were walking, you wondered what was in the envelope. It didn't look official—it was in a personal envelope with just her name on it. You realized that in his haste to catch you before you left, Deffens forgot to make sure the seal was fixed and the flap had come open. You couldn't help yourself—you looked inside to find that it contained five

$10 bills with a single note: "Armstrong." It clicked in your mind that *Armstrong* was the case that Deffens had just received as an appointment, so the money was probably a type of kickback.

Later, you confront Deffens with it, and he tells you that if you want to go into the legal field, you had better take off your rose-colored glasses and wake up to the real world.

"Everybody does it, sweet pea," he said in a tone that was patiently patronizing.

"Judge Townshend's wife works for Judge Harris, who pays her $75,000 a year for two days a week of half-assed work. Judge Ridgeland has a side business with Tom Skinner, and he gets probably 65% of his appointments—is that a coincidence? I buy the judges lunch and take them with me to my box seats at NASCAR and basketball so they don't 'forget' me when they appoint. Judge Townshend appointed his cousin to a guardian *at litem* case and approved the $200,000 bill that the guy submitted for watching out for the interests of the minor child—even though there was no family conflict and it was a simple case establishing a trust. Judge Anderson lets Julie make the appointments so I slip her $50—that's a lot cheaper than the other judges and it's not half as bad as the other things that go on around here."

Your faith in the process is shaken, and the whole thing seems sleazy to you. On the other hand, it doesn't necessarily affect the client, since Deffens seems to do a good job. So where's the harm, especially if everyone is doing it?

Questions for Discussion

1. What, if anything, do you plan to do about your knowledge?
2. Is it much worse to pay someone for appointments than to "butter them up" with false flattery?
3. Is there a better way to provide for indigent legal services than the appointment method?

8

Brothers and Law

"What did he do this time?" you ask as your wife hands you the phone. Her brother is calling—and whenever he calls, you know it is because he needs money or is in trouble.

Sure enough, it turns out that he has been arrested for assault. He and a neighbor began arguing over an overhanging tree and, fueled by more than a few beers, fists started flying and so did a few pieces of lawn furniture. Now he is in lockup and needs someone to bail him out.

You are a defense attorney and very familiar with the jail and process. It takes less than an hour to get him out, although you are now on the hook for his bail money. Obviously, he wants you to defend him against what he called "this bull**** charge," and you wearily agree, knowing that you could do nothing else since you'd bear the wrath of your wife if you refused.

"The guy ended up with 36 stitches. I don't think it's a trivial matter," argued Correy Mann, the prosecutor who was assigned the case. "In fact, I may go with aggravated, since the chair could be considered a weapon."

"Oh come on, that's stretching it. At most, it's a misdemeanor worth a fine. In fact, it could be self defense—both were swinging."

"Uh, you better talk to your client again." Correy looked up at him with the file spread in front of her. "The police report says that the victim was on the ground covering his head when your guy was hammering him with the lawn chair."

"That's one guy's word against another. What about witnesses?" You knew you should have picked up the police report before going in to see her.

"Says there are some. Anyway, no go on a fine—we are going to bump it up. Sorry, Matt." She knew that the client was related to him.

"Man, that a**hole needed a beating for a long time." Your brother-in-law was blithely unaware of the seriousness of having felony charges pending against him. He was the baby of the family and had always had someone pulling him out of trouble. Small, slight, with long blond hair, he looked more like a girl or a teenager than the 28-year-old man he was. It was hard to believe that he had enough gumption to actually swing a chair, since he rarely did anything more active than go down to the corner for his daily case of beer.

"The fact is that if you were not in fear of immediate harm, you cannot hit someone over the head with a metal chair."

You cannot get it through his head that he could be looking at prison time since he did have several priors for drunk driving and one for resisting arrest. It looks like there are three witnesses that are willing to testify that your brother-in-law hit the man with no provocation other than the argument. They were all relatives of the victim, however, so you think that if he was defending himself, you could impugn their credibility without much problem.

"So, man, like, if I say I was afraid of him, everything would be ok?" The wheels in your brother-in-law's brain moved slowly, but they were finally moving.

"I'm saying that at least we'd have a legal defense to start with."

"OK, then, sure, I was afraid of him, he was bigger than me, you know and, uh, he was starting to come toward me. Does that sound right?"

"I can't tell you what to say. I can tell you that without self-defense, we have nothing and I can't guarantee that you won't end up in prison."

"Well, then, ok, that's what happened."

You are relatively sure that he's lying. You also know that he wouldn't survive prison and your marriage wouldn't survive it if you lost the case. On the other hand, you don't know how the witnesses may come across or whether there might be more evidence to support the victim's story that the attack was unprovoked. Obviously, suborning perjury is a crime and an ethical violation, but you know that most defense attorneys wouldn't be taking many cases to trial if they didn't interpret those rules somewhat loosely. You also wonder how Correy and the other prosecutors will treat you if you put him up on the stand and his story is torn to shreds.

Questions for Discussion

1. What should you do, knowing that your brother-in-law may be committing perjury? Would your answer be any different if it were just a court-appointed client?
2. If you didn't allow it, what would be your options?
3. What should be the goal of defense attorneys who are defending guilty clients? How many attorneys do you think allow clients to lie on the stand?

9

Probation or Prison?

You could have been in the same situation yourself. Instead, it is Mary Lee Smith, one of your probationers, who is about to stand before the judge in a probation revocation hearing.

When you and your husband split ten years ago, you had two children and eventually had to declare bankruptcy and accept food stamps to be able to pay the rent. After seven years working as a secretary at the nearby state juvenile corrections center, receiving constant encouragement from Mrs. Jones, the superintendent, and taking advantage of a criminal justice scholarship program, you finished a degree in administration of justice and qualified for an entry-level position with the community resources division of the state department of corrections. You advanced as the system grew and now, three years later, you are a probation supervisor in Judge Longworth's court.

In a way, Mary Lee is as much a victim as she is an offender. Married at seventeen, she quit high school and moved west with her husband, who was in the army. By the time she was twenty, she had two children and was divorced. With babysitters to pay and skills that would command no more than minimum wage, Mary Lee turned to such income supplements as shoplifting, bad check writing, and occasionally prostitution. Her check-passing skills developed rapidly, and it was not long before she had amassed a series of convictions, not to mention several lesser offenses for petty larceny that were disposed of by the prosecutor's declaration of *nolle prosequi*. To date, Mary Lee has not served a day in prison. Judge Longworth has used admonition, restitution, suspended sentence, and probation in efforts to rehabilitate Mary Lee. However, Mary Lee's criminal conduct has persisted, as has her inability to stretch her food stamps, welfare payments, and part-time minimum-wage employment into a satisfactory existence for herself and her children. To complicate matters, the welfare safety net that had helped keep Mary Lee and her children afloat would cease to exist for her within 24 months.

Judge Longworth has called you into his chambers before the hearing. He read your violation report with interest. You pointed out Mary Lee's family obligations and the imminent possibility that the children would have to be placed in foster homes if she were confined. You also pointed out that she has been faithful in making restitution and that she maintains a regular church relationship and a satisfactory home environment for her children. Although your report is fair and accurate, you realize that the judge has sensed your own misgivings and uncertainty concerning Mary Lee.

Judge Longworth looks up from your report and comes directly to the point. "Do you really believe this woman deserves to go back into the community? You certainly seem to have found some redeeming features in her conduct that I don't," he says. "Unfortunately, it appears to me that the only way she is going to learn to respect other people's property is to be deprived of her own freedom. I think the community is getting pretty tired of this kind of repetitive criminal conduct." Judge Longworth looks to you expectantly for an answer.

You are on the spot. You know your answer might put Mary Lee in the penitentiary or give her another chance on probation. The judge will make up his own mind, but you know he values your opinion.

Questions for Discussion

1. Should Mary Lee be sent to prison or allowed to remain on probation?
2. Is there anything else you can do as a probation officer to help Mary Lee make a more successful adjustment regarding living within the limits of the law?
3. Is it enough for the courts or society to tell someone like Mary Lee not to commit petty larceny, or does our system have a moral duty to provide her with support services that could increase her chance of success?

10

"My Job Is to Defend the Constitution"

Most of your clients are kind of pathetic. They have broken the law, sure, but they don't seem to be especially evil or even competent at their lawbreaking. When friends and family ask you how you can defend guilty people, you always answer with the same well-worn retort that you've heard since law school—that you are defending the Constitution as much as you are defending an individual, and that the system works because someone is looking out for the rights of the accused. However, that phrase seems to stick in your throat when you think of Charlie Simmons.

Simmons was a court-appointed case, and you met him in the small room in the jail reserved for attorney visits. He is not a pleasant man. In fact, the way he scornfully looked you up and down and then focused in on you—much as a predator stares at their prey before they strike—made you downright nervous. You didn't sense any compassion, fear, kinship, or humanity in him. Although you have never been very imaginative or emotional, you could sense that Charlie Simmons could easily kill someone and calmly eat a sandwich right afterwards. He was scary.

Simmons had been arrested and charged with an armed robbery, attempted murder, and rape. Allegedly, he had stopped a young couple as they were walking late at night down by the river that runs through the downtown area. He forced them into a deserted section of the riverwalk area, cold-cocked the guy with the butt of his gun, and then raped the girl. He might have killed them both if a river police patrol hadn't happened to be going down the river about that time and scared him off. The couple was rescued but was so traumatized that they couldn't make any positive identification of their attacker. He was caught because the DNA from his semen was matched through the government DNA database. His DNA was already in the system from a previous rape.

"As I explained the first time we met, the DNA evidence is very damaging. In most cases, the jury is likely to base their decision largely upon the scientific evidence. I think your best chance is to make a plea bargain for reduced prison time," you had counseled Simmons.

You had found it hard to meet his eyes. You could feel he was staring, challenging you to look up at him and meet his gaze. After a few sections of silence you did look up, and his expression was malevolent.

"I'm not pleading. You're supposed to help me, so do your g**d*** job."

"I am supposed to represent you—not work miracles." A spark of anger at his attitude had fueled your response. "If you have any information that can aid in your defense, let me hear about it."

"I did those kids so I don't exactly have an alibi," he had responded lazily, amused at your reaction.

"Then I think that if you insist on going to trial, the only thing we can do is to undermine the validity of the match—that's the only evidence the prosecution will present anyway."

You had a sick feeling in your stomach, knowing that you were attempting to acquit a confessed rapist, yet you couldn't see what else you were supposed to do.

Later that week, in the restroom of the courthouse, you hear a whispered conversation. It is obvious that the whisperers do not know that someone else is within hearing distance of their murmurs. From what you hear, it becomes clear that the city's crime lab has been having some problems. The two individuals mention that the lab director does not have a license that he is supposed to have, and there have been irregularities in the way that evidence has been stored, leading to an upcoming investigation. The information has not hit the newspapers yet, and you are relatively sure that it will be kept under wraps until the investigation begins, which won't occur for another month.

You ponder what, if anything, you could do with this information, and then it hits you like a brick: this could mean that Charlie Simmons might walk free. If you found out a little more, you could cross-examine the forensic examiner, using the knowledge to undercut the integrity of the testing and matching of Simmons's DNA. All you need is reasonable doubt and you can probably get him off, especially since the victims are not going to be able to I.D. him. If the defendant was anyone other than Simmons, you wouldn't give a second thought to the plan, but you know that he is guilty as sin. You believe with certainty that he would do it again, maybe killing someone next time. No one knows about the crime lab's problems yet, and when the scandal does come out, it is possible that Simmons could use it for an appeal—you just wouldn't have to be his attorney. You wish you'd never heard the information, because now you have to decide what to do with it.

Questions for Discussion

1. What is the ethical course of action? What does the law and legal ethics dictate in this situation?

2. Do you think there are clients for whom defense attorneys don't work as hard to defend as they do others? How do most attorneys resolve the fact that they are defending guilty criminals?
3. What are the limits of a zealous defense?

11

A Question of Integrity

Sheryl Tucker twirled her hair between her fingers as she contemplated the keyboard. The Word document on her computer screen was a letter she had written to the chief of police and sheriff in the small southern jurisdiction in which she was the elected district attorney. Generally she had a pretty easy life, as normally there were no major cases that came across her desk other than the rare domestic homicide. Of smaller crimes, her county saw the standard assortment of assaults, burglaries, DWIs, and others that were usually plea bargained rather than taken to trial. Still, she had five prosecutors working under her and the court was fairly active in the ordinary course of the week.

Today, however, her task was not ordinary and she was trying to figure out how to navigate the waters of small-town politics and the law. Recently, a sheriff's deputy and a city police officer had both been fired for lying. The sheriff's deputy had lied on his job application about a prior arrest a dozen years before, and the city police officer had lied to the chief about a use-of-force incident that, unfortunately for him, had been captured on his dashboard camera. Both officers took their cases to arbitration as was their right, and in both cases the arbitrator ruled that firing was too harsh a punishment, ordering that the officers be reinstated. She knew of these incidents because, in a town this size, everyone knew everything about everyone who was associated with the courthouse. The gossip mill was more effective than *Access Hollywood* in getting the news out, and the cases had been reported in the newspaper as well.

The letter on her screen informed the two law enforcement agencies that she no longer could or would prosecute any case for which either officer would have to testify as a witness for the prosecution. She explained that according to the *Brady v. Maryland* case, prosecutors are obligated to turn over exculpatory evidence to the defense when asked, and that evidence of officer-witness credibility would be subject to a *Brady* motion. Defense attorneys could always say that the officer was lying on the stand because he had lied in the past. She saw no way that the officers could ever be testifying witnesses for her again, regardless of the case or their role. Yet she knew that the chief and sheriff would be stuck between a rock and a hard place because their budgets did not allow them to keep an officer to open doors or answer phones; they probably needed these guys out on the street. Still, she was bound by the law and her conscience; and she knew that these two men, because of their actions, were worthless to her as prosecution witnesses.

As she expected, the letter had set off a whirlwind of consternation and anger. The sheriff put his deputy on suspension again and was trying to find a way to appeal the arbitration decision. In the meantime, the lawyer for the deputy was telling the press that he was going to sue Sheryl for interference of contract and that she had no right to tell the sheriff that the deputy couldn't testify, which was basically part of his job. "She doesn't know how juries would react," he said. "Her speculation is putting a man's career in jeopardy." The police chief basically said that he couldn't afford to bench the officer and that he was still on patrol.

As luck would have it, the city police officer in question pulled over a man who was driving above the speed limit through the area on the interstate. The man consented to a search of his car, and the officer found drugs and drug paraphernalia in the pocket of a jacket on the back seat. The man was charged with possession with intent to sell because of the amount, and he was facing some pretty substantial prison time so he wouldn't plead, even for reduced prison time. His lawyer, who was from another town, had been in Sheryl's office several times and made it clear he thought that he was above the caliber of the prosecutors he would be facing if the case went to trial. She knew the case hinged on the consent. The officer said the man consented to the search, and now the guy is saying he didn't consent. If it were any other officer, Sheryl would have no problem taking the case to trial, knowing she'd get a conviction. Juries are almost always going to believe officers over drug-carrying defendants. The problem was that Sheryl had said she was not going to use this officer as a witness. If he couldn't testify, she basically had no case.

The other wrinkle in the case was that, since the lawyer was from out of town, he did not know of the officer's past as the local attorneys would have. Also, because he wasn't quite as smart as he thought he was, he forgot to file a *Brady* motion, meaning that he didn't ask for exculpatory information. Arguably, Sheryl was legally obligated to give him something only when he asked for it. Legally she might be OK in keeping the information about the officer from the attorney. Ethically, she knew she probably ought to at least share it with him, if not drop the case entirely. On the other hand, it may be true what the attorney said: She was only speculating that juries would not believe the officer in this case; or they might not even care if he was lying since the drugs were found. Sheryl also wondered how she would be perceived if she backtracked on what she had said in the letter and now decided to use the officer as a witness. Time was running out for her to decide, since the trial was scheduled to begin and she needed to submit the witness list.

Questions for Discussion

1. Should you go to trial using the officer as a witness? If so, should you turn over the information about the officers to the defense attorney?
2. What is the prosecutor's role in the criminal justice system?
3. How do you think you will be perceived if you drop the case? How will you be perceived if you do use the officer as a witness?

12

Conflicting Duties

As a defense attorney, you usually can find some redeeming characteristics about your clients. Often they are guilty of something less than the charges filed, or there are extenuating circumstances, or some other reason makes it easy to try to help them escape the heavy hand of the justice system. Today you are scheduled to see a client who seems to have no redeeming qualities. Simon Cook is a predator and probably a psychopath. He is on trial for attempted murder because he tried to run down an ex-girlfriend with his car. He saw her coming out of a bar with another man and headed straight for them. The man jumped back into the bar, but the woman ran down the street with Cook right behind her, veering the car onto the sidewalk as often as he could in pursuit. If she had run a little slower or there had been fewer telephone poles and trash cans he had to avoid, she probably would have been dead. Your case is based on intent with the argument that he didn't intend to kill her, only scare her. It might even be true.

As you went over Cook's testimony, you couldn't shake the feeling that he was actually amused by the whole process. Finally you say to him, "Look, it is very possible that you will be seeing the inside of prison again. I know you've been in before on an aggravated assault charge, but that was only for a year. This time you could be looking at a lot longer." He had a record that included robberies and assaults, and you suspected he had done a lot more. "Maybe you should have left your ex alone."

Cook leaned back in his chair and said, "She needed to be taught a lesson. I have to teach people not to disrespect me. Anyway, I'm sure I'll convince the jury I didn't mean anything. I'm pretty lucky about these things." He had a smirkey little grin on his face and you had to ask what he meant by that last statement.

"This attorney-client thing—you can't tell anybody anything I tell you, right?" Cook asked in response to your question. You answered, "That's right. I can't violate your privilege, and anything you say must remain confidential."

"Well, this isn't the first time I had a woman who needed a lesson. Ten years ago, I accidentally killed a girl I was dating because she made me mad. She was an uppity little slut and I didn't mean to kill her, just mess her up a little, but she died. But some other guy she was seeing got the blame. They didn't even know about me. Anyway, he's up in State now—doing life. I've got the good luck, he's got the bad. That's life, I guess. Poor slob." He chuckled as he finished the story.

"What's his name?" you asked, without really knowing why, since there was not much you could legally do about the information. "You can't tell anybody, right?" Cook abruptly stopped leaning back in the chair and leaned toward you, staring intently into your eyes, and you realized how dangerous the man was. "No. Unfortunately for the guy, there is nothing I can do for him without endangering your interests," you responded, trying not to let Cook know how uncomfortable he made you feel.

"Well, that's good then. Name is Jim Sullivan. I even ran into him on my agg bit. I almost told him that he was in there for me, but didn't 'cos I didn't want the headache of watching for him to stick a shiv in my back or something." That grin became even wider.

"I don't suppose there is any way I could convince you to come forward and admit the crime so that Sullivan could be freed. It would be the right thing to do." You groaned inwardly at your Pollyannaish statement, and Cook actually laughed.

"Hey buddy, if I did the right thing all the time, I wouldn't need you, would I?"

After Cook had gone, you sat there and pondered what you could or should do with the information that some guy named Jim Sullivan is in prison for a crime he did not commit. He is not your client so you don't owe him a duty as a legal professional, but your heart tells you that you owe him something simply as a human being and an officer of the court. You really have no idea what to do in this situation and even calling up your old mentor and law partner could be construed as a breach of confidence. Telling the prosecutor about the case and Sullivan's innocence would alert them to suspect one of your clients if they even listened to you at all. You don't have any evidence other than Cook's statement anyway. You wish someone would tell you what to do.

Questions for Discussion

1. Does the attorney-client privilege overcome an innocent person's right to not be incarcerated for a crime he or she did not commit?
2. Is there any way to reveal the information without compromising the interests of the client?
3. Would the bar association punish a defense attorney who came forward with this type of information? If they would, should they?

13

See No Evil?

You stopped at this small roadside café 35 miles outside of the city because you were simply too tired to go on without some food and coffee in your system. You catch yourself staring at your food, wondering how many calories are in the hamburger and fries. You are exhausted and hungry and decide you don't care if there are 2,000 calories—you deserve it.

The last several weeks have been nothing but nonstop work and stress. Building a legal defense practice is never easy, but it's especially difficult these days. The recession has affected everyone, and the trickle-down effect has hit even the lowly echelons of criminal defense. The "big dog" law firms are hurting and, thus, are picking up cases they wouldn't have bothered with before, even soliciting appointments from judges, which means that there have been fewer cases to go around for sole practitioners such as yourself. You've hustled to get the cases you've got and some of them are stinkers.

Like the Harris case. This case is why you are returning from the state prison where you had to interview a person who was supposed to have information that would be beneficial to your client, but it was a bust. The individual merely knew someone who knew someone who knew someone who might have heard something about someone else who had something to do with the armed robbery that your client was charged with. Whether or not he really did hear something about the case was impossible to tell. When you went to law school, you never expected that you would have to be part-time investigator, part-time counselor, and full-time underpaid and overworked defense attorney. The game seemed to be rigged from the start with some defense attorneys getting most of the easy appointments and hobnobbing with the judges. You weren't in the "in" club, and you wondered if you ever would be. Now, you are looking at probably 4 or 5 hours of work back in your office.

As you finish up the last of the fries, a couple in a back booth catches your attention. The man's back was to you and he was leaning toward his companion, nibbling at her ear. "Gross," you think to yourself, "Get a room, buddy." Then you almost gag on your french fry—it's Judge Roberts! And that definitely isn't his wife. In fact, it is a prosecutor. You realize that you are witnessing a late afternoon tryst and, what makes it worse, the two are involved in a very high-profile case right now. A doctor is being prosecuted for the alleged murder of his wife. The case is going to be hard to prove because there is no good evidence. She died of a virus, and the prosecution's case was that the virus was created by the doctor in a lab and introduced to her through infected food. When she got sick, he didn't take her to the hospital but instead waited for her to die. The defense is arguing that the forensic tests used were problematic and the expert used by the prosecution was not well thought of in the scientific community. Everyone was waiting for the judge's ruling as to whether the test that supposedly proved the virus was man-made was going to be admitted. And here was the judge, nibbling on the ear of the prosecutor! While it is not illegal for judges and prosecutors to have relationships, it is a conflict of interest when a judge has a secret affair with a prosecutor! The defense attorney in the case could probably use it for an appeal if the judge ruled against the defense.

You stand up and stroll to the restroom right past the couple. When they look up at you, you act surprised and say, "Oh, hello, I didn't expect to see anyone I knew here in this place." Inwardly, you are amused at the flustered and guilty looks they pass to each other as they return your greeting. They know you know that you have information that could be very detrimental to their reputations and careers. You leave the restaurant and wonder what course of action you should take. You could tell the defense attorney, you could report it to the head administrative judge in the district, you could do nothing, you could visit the prosecutor tomorrow and discuss one of your cases with her that needed a plea deal, and/or you could visit the judge and ask him if he had any appointments for you. Somehow you think that your prospects might be looking up, depending, of course, on how you play it.

Questions for Discussion

1. Should you use the information to your own advantage or report the couple's affair?
2. Is there a downside to reporting what you saw to the defense attorney in the other case?
3. What should the judge and/or prosecutor do at this point?

Section III

ETHICS AND CORRECTIONS

The impact of ethical considerations can be observed in both community and institutional correctional settings. The moral duty to victims of crime, the protection and security of communities where citizens work and live, just consequences for those persons who commit crimes, and the moral responsibility to maintain custody of offenders in safe institutional environments all comprise important ethical concerns and challenges.

How do the legal requirements for our justice process square with ethical challenges to make the system more just? For example, charges of discrimination based on race or economic status need to be addressed when considering sentencing of those who are convicted of crimes. And what is the purpose of our justice system—to send offenders to prison "as" punishment, or "for" punishment? Should we try to reform or rehabilitate prison inmates, or make living conditions in prison as harsh and austere as the law will allow?

Probation, parole, and other community corrections programs supervise offenders in community settings. Ethical issues in these environments include victims' rights and the impact of support services and financial fees on offenders under community supervision. Restorative justice, a relatively recent justice initiative, has demonstrated some promise in addressing victim needs and citizen concerns along with offender responsibility and potential restoration to the community. What are the ethical implications of a process by which victims can express to offenders the damage they have experienced and the offender has the chance to express genuine remorse and to offer some form of restitution? At the other end of the spectrum looms the dilemma of supervision fees, imposed on offenders by the state and to an even greater extent by private probation agencies. Although it seems only fair that offenders pay for a portion of the cost of their supervision, fees may represent a substantial financial burden for many offenders who struggle to provide adequate support for themselves and their families.

Does the community itself bear any ethical responsibility to give offenders a second chance once their sentence has been completed? Should social and religious institutions reach out to ex-offenders? What about prospective employers?

Only about 27 percent of persons incarcerated are convicted of violent offenses. Others are convicted and sentenced for such crimes as burglary and substance abuse. Politics and public opinion often play a role in who goes to prison and for how long. One example involves the long-standing debate regarding why crack cocaine (which is generally used by the poor and by racial minorities) has a more severe penalty than does powdered cocaine (which tends to be a drug of choice for the more affluent members of society).

Prison conditions comprise a variety of ethical challenges for law-makers, corrections administrators, and officers. Safety issues abound, including victimization of some inmates by other inmates who are sexual predators. Adequate health care is another issue that is particularly relevant in prisons where overcrowding is a problem. For example, there are indications that tuberculosis is on the increase in such environments. Access to psychological treatment, vocational training, and education programs are also concerns of inmates and prison staff. The age-old question: "What do the undeserving deserve?" resonates with moral meaning.

The legal rights of prisoners have evolved from the time of a "hands-off" doctrine where they had no rights and were at the mercy of the prison warden and guards to modern times where the right to legal aid, religious beliefs, visitation privileges, personal safety, and adequate medical and health care have been established. Popular movies such as *Cool Hand Luke* and *The Shawshank Redemption* accurately depict the era of the hands-off doctrine.

Another growing ethical dilemma rises from the graying of our society's prison population. Our prison system is seeing a rapid increase in the numbers of prisoners in their sixties, seventies, and eighties. Older prisoners have more health-related problems than do younger inmates. These problems require more sophisticated and more expensive long-term care. Older prisoners who have been incarcerated for a decade or longer also find it very difficult, if not impossible, to adjust to life outside of prison. In addition, other categories of inmates such as women, juveniles, and "special needs" offenders (with mental or physical disabilities) further strain limited corrections resources.

Privatization

Private corporations such as Corrections Corporation of America (CCA) have contracted with states to run private prisons, arguing that they can operate and manage prisons more efficiently and effectively. A number of ethical issues arise: Should states relinquish their responsibility to supervise offenders and protect communities to private business?

Should private corporations be allowed to profit from human suffering? A number of concerns have emerged regarding privatization of corrections, including poor correctional officer morale, escapes, increases in prison violence, and various forms of corruption. While some privatized community and institutional corrections operations seem to be fulfilling their promise of efficiency, effectiveness, and accountability, many others appear to have fallen short of their initial claims.

The Death Penalty

Perhaps there is no corrections issue more burdened by moral debate than the death penalty. One might pose the question: Should there even be a death penalty? It is interesting that both those in favor of and those against the death penalty can offer moral arguments based on religious belief and documentation.

Discrimination, racial bias, and arbitrariness are often raised as points of debate regarding the death penalty. For example, one problem is that black defendant/white victim cases are more likely to result in the death penalty than black defendant/black victim cases. Another even more troubling aspect is the number of persons on death row who are now being found innocent on the basis of DNA testing. In the past, an untold number of innocent people may have been executed for crimes they did not commit. Former Governor George Ryan of Illinois placed a moratorium on executions because of his doubts concerning the veracity of evidence in a number of death row cases.

There are strong moral/ethical arguments offered both in support of the death penalty and against it. Since human beings are not perfect and on occasion make mistakes, it is hard to imagine that our justice system does not also make mistakes from time to time. Is there such a thing as a reasonable number of mistakes regarding the administration of the death penalty?

Corrections is an area full of ethical responsibilities and moral challenges. From concerns for victim rights and humane treatment of inmates to a just death penalty policy, the consequences of ethical choices in corrections are substantial and of lasting significance.

Suggestions for Further Reading

Braswell, M., Fuller, J., & Lozoff, B. (2001). *Corrections, peacemaking and restorative justice*. Cincinnati, OH: LexisNexis/Anderson.

Braswell, M., Miller, L., & Cabana, D. (2006). *Human relations and corrections* (5th ed.). Long Grove, IL: Waveland Press.

Cabana, D. (1996). *Death at midnight: The confession of an executioner.* Boston: Northeastern University Press.

Clear, T. (1994). *Harm in American penology: Offenders, victims and their communities.* Albany: State University of New York Press.

Conover, T. (2000). *Newjack: Guarding Sing Sing*. New York: Random House.

Conrad, J. (1982). What do the undeserving deserve? In R. Johnson and H. Toch (Eds.), *The pains of imprisonment* (pp. 313–330). Beverly Hills, CA: Sage.
Haas, K., & Alpert, G. (2006). *The dilemmas of corrections* (5th ed.) Long Grove, IL: Waveland Press.
Hassine, V. (2004). *Life without parole: Living in prison today* (3rd ed.). Los Angeles: Roxbury Press.
Hickey, J., & Scharf, P. (1980). *Toward a just correctional system.* San Francisco: Jossey-Bass.
Jones, D. (2006). *Humane prisons*. Boston: Blackwell.
Kleinig, J. (2001). *Discretion, community and correctional ethics*. Lanham, MD: Rowman & Littlefield.
Kleinig, J. (2006). *Correctional ethics: The international library of essay in public and professional ethics*. United Kingdom: Ashgate.
Kratcoski, P. C. (2004). *Correctional counseling and treatment* (5th ed.). Long Grove, IL: Waveland Press.
Quinn, J. F. (2003). *Corrections: A concise introduction* (2nd ed.). Long Grove, IL: Waveland Press.
Sykes, G. (1958). *The society of captives: A study of a maximum security prison*. Princeton, NJ: Princeton University Press.
Whitehead, J., Pollock, J., & Braswell, M. (2003). *Exploring corrections.* Cincinnati, OH: LexisNexis/Anderson.

1

The Limits of Responsibility

"Hey, Mark, bring me one of those cigars," you shout, pouring yourself another steaming cup of coffee.

You, Frank, Mark, and Ted had been coming to your lake cottage every Thursday night for the last ten years. Located just thirty minutes from Middleville where you all live, it is a great place to get away. Who says middle-aged men can't have their own clubhouse? Sometimes you drink tea and soft drinks; other times you and the boys might have a couple of beers. When it was cold, hot coffee tended to be the preferred drink. Whatever the beverage of choice, your evenings together always culminated with the four of you smoking cigars and talking about whatever came to mind. On this particularly cold February night, you perked, drank, smoked, and talked.

"My real estate business has been mighty good to me," you say. "My wife and children are healthy and happy. I've got a lot to be thankful for."

"I'll second that thought," Mark echoes. "My hardware store has held its own, and Sue has recovered from her surgery."

Ted, a successful local attorney, reflects on his past year of getting through a difficult case and being able to breathe again. It has also been a pretty good year for Frank, a third-generation cattle farmer.

You continue, "You know, I've been thinking about those homeless folks on the streets this winter. Seems like there are more of them than ever before. And that piece in the paper about the need for a women's shelter. I've been wondering if, with me being so fortunate, maybe I ought to see about helping those folks in some way."

Casually blowing spiraling smoke rings, Mark replies, "God helps those who help themselves."

Frank chimes in, "Don't go getting bleeding-heart liberal on us, Rick. I'd like to see some of those homeless men out on my farm working like I do. Besides, everyone knows a lot of the homeless are just lazy—and as for the women's shelter, they need to take shelter in their own homes and be good mothers and wives."

"I don't know," you reply. "It's awful cold out there. Everyone's not as lucky as we are. I've been thinking about calling Jenny Andrews, the community director of social services, to see if she could use a couple of my empty buildings downtown."

Relighting his cigar, Ted compliments you for your charitable attitude and adds, "Just remember, Rick, the downtrodden have to want to help themselves. And no matter how many you help, there are always others to take their place. Besides, you need to consider liability issues. No matter how good your intentions are, some people will sue you at the drop of a hat."

"Maybe so, but it seems like we ought to do our part and give something back to our community," you protest.

"We do," Mark replies. "We pay taxes and give to charities like the United Way and March of Dimes."

"Come on, Rick, lighten up," Frank chides.

You smile sheepishly, "OK, but is there something else we could do?"

Questions for Discussion

1. Does Rick have a point, or should he just let human service agencies take care of problems associated with homelessness or victims of abuse?
2. How might citizen involvement proactively help police with issues regarding the homeless and abuse victims?
3. Do those of us who are financially comfortable have a duty toward others? If so, what is that duty?

2

The Minister and the Ex-Offender

As one of your community's leading ministers, you have always spoken out for progressive correctional reform. Your congregation has usually backed you, and on the few occasions when they did not, they still remained tolerant of your views. Now, however, things are different. Sally, a former member of your church, was once active in working with the church youth. She has since been convicted of embezzlement from the local bank where she worked and sentenced to a year in prison.

As her minister, you kept in contact with her from the beginning of her imprisonment. No one ever really believed she would have to serve time; since the money was returned, no one expected that her boss would even bring charges against her. Everyone has financial burdens at one time or another, and Sally had experienced a succession of problems over a long period of time. The clincher was her husband's permanent disability as a result of an accident. The bills began to pile up faster than she could get them paid. They had mortgaged their house and sold one of their two cars. Finally, in desperation, Sally "borrowed" several thousand dollars from the bank where she had worked as a teller for years. When her crime was discovered, her world crumbled around her.

She has now returned to the community after serving a prison term for embezzlement. When you talked to her the day after she returned, you realized that she was a broken woman. Her daughter had dropped out of school to care for the father, and his disability check was their primary source of income. You counseled her and encouraged her to try and regain her place in the community. You also helped her find work and even suggested that she return to your church, where she had previously been very active. She was reluctant to rejoin the church, fearing rejection by the congregation. You tried to reassure her that everyone was behind her and wanted her to return. In fact, a substantial number of the congregation members had told you as much. When you learned that there would soon be an opening in the Sunday school for a youth director, you asked Sally to consider taking the position. After several days of thinking about it, she agreed.

You have now brought her name before the Sunday school committee and they have, to a person, refused to consider her for the youth leader position. Their bitterness has taken you totally by surprise; their words remain all too clear in your mind: "How would it look to the rest of the community to have an ex-convict directing our youth?" Should you fight for what you believe is right and risk dissension, or should you tell Sally that her fears are more valid than you had thought; that her former fellow church members have not been able to forgive and forget?

Questions for Discussion

1. What are some contradictions between church members' attitude toward helping the less fortunate and their actions?
2. What role does the minister play in this case?
3. Could he have done anything differently?

3

Temporary Release

You are the lieutenant in charge of a section of the state's maximum-security penitentiary. Because you are in a sparsely populated Midwestern state, your inmate population is not that large and the "lifers" you have to supervise are, for the most part, dedicated to coping with the daily routine. When there is a problem, it is usually major, but fortunately that doesn't happen very often. It is a well-kept secret that a security job in a well-run maximum security institution is often a lot less challenging than at other institutions with inmates convicted of lesser offenses in medium security.

Shorty Smith is a good example. Convicted of capital murder in a state that does not have the death penalty, Shorty will spend life without parole in this institution; he will die in prison one way or another. His only other possibility would be to move to a group geriatric facility, if he lives to age 70 or becomes terminally ill. Otherwise, he will stay right where he is for the rest of his life.

Shorty's crime was an armed robbery of a convenience store, culminating in a fight for his knife by the cashier and resulting in the death of the cashier. Shorty was not particularly remorseful, just mad at his bad luck and at the stupidity of a cashier who would grapple with an armed assailant over $129.37. Shorty, of course, wasn't one to back away from any confrontation—in fact, the only real disciplinary problem with Shorty was control of a hair-trigger temper and the possession of a cell-made "shank." The last one was made from a plastic hair brush, complete with a blood groove and serrated blade. Yes, Shorty was dangerous, but in maximum security he was easy to control.

Maybe one of the reasons Shorty was no more than an occasional problem was that he had a devoted mother who had visited him every two weeks since he was convicted. Mrs. Opperman, Shorty's mother, said she always loved Shorty because his father was her first love, but he had left her as soon as he found out she was pregnant. Although she tried hard to raise Shorty in a decent, "Christian" manner, it was hard to do with her overscheduled duties as a hostess at the Magic Bar and Grill.

So Shorty mostly reared himself, and now that it was too late to do anything about it, she felt it was her motherly duty to visit him as often as the prison regulations would permit.

Mrs. Opperman was on her way to the prison for a special Christmas visit when she was mugged while boarding the bus. She was so traumatized by the event that she went into ventricular fibrillation and died at the scene. Shorty was outraged. "What kind of animal would assault an old woman like that?" Shorty shouted. Then Shorty got the message—straight from God, some said: Since an armed mugging was an aggravated assault, and a statutory addition to the state's felony-murder rule, if the attacker was ever identified, he would likely be sent to Shorty's prison.

Shorty has begged for a temporary release to go home to attend his mother's funeral, but you could not, in all good conscience, recommend it. Even shackled and under armed guard, Shorty could still be dangerous. Besides, the colonel who ran the security division has told you that with all the vacationing custodial personnel for the upcoming Christmas holidays, he could not spare a guard for a day and a half, even if Shorty's family would pay the costs. With Shorty's anger growing by the hour, his family decided to hire a lawyer. You were interviewed by the warden regarding Shorty's behavior and you said in no uncertain terms that, dead mother or not, Shorty is dangerous, more so now than before, and he ought not to be released for any reason, even under double guard.

The family lawyer sued and got an early hearing because Shorty's mother's body needed to be buried. Shorty's family lawyer alleged that it was cruel and unusual punishment—a violation of Shorty's Eighth Amendment rights—to deny Shorty access to his mother's funeral, particularly when the family would pay for any expenses occurred. You, the warden, and the Commissioner of Corrections were all named as defendants in the lawsuit. The warden reiterated your statement as to Shorty's potential for danger, and the rest is history. It has been all over the news media about the corrections department denying Shorty his "constitutional right" to see his beloved mother put to rest. The irony that Shorty's mother was killed in an incident similar to the one in which Shorty had killed the convenience store cashier was never a part of the story.

You wait uneasily for the judge's reaction to the lawsuit. If Shorty made it out, you would lose the respect of all the other inmates; if he did not, he would have to stay locked down for a long time. And who knows, Shorty's mother's assailant may eventually end up in the same prison. Both Shorty and the assailant would have a lifetime to await the pleasure of each other's company. Right now, a medium-security prison didn't look like such a bad place to work.

QUESTIONS FOR DISCUSSION

1. Does denying Shorty the right to attend his mother's funeral violate standards of "normal human decency?"
2. Are there alternative ways to help Shorty deal with the loss of his mother?

4

Six Months to Go

Six months ago the biggest concern in your life was finishing college. Now your biggest concern is your own personal safety. Never in a million years did you dream that you would be spending the twentieth year of your life in a state prison. As a sociology major in college you studied about crime, criminals, and prisons, but that was nothing compared to your situation now. The constant noise of steel and concrete; the smell of bodies, cigarettes, and old buildings; the inability to go where you want to go, eat what you want to eat—all this is foreign and confusing to you.

Sure, you smoked some grass and sometimes used pills to stay up and study for exams when you were in college; a lot of other students did the same. You had never expected to get "busted" for selling a small amount of marijuana and uppers to an acquaintance who turned out to be a narcotics officer. But you did. Since it was your first offense, your lawyer said probation was a sure thing. Unfortunately for you, however, you got a judge who was fed up with drug abuse. He decided that it was time to crack down, and he used you as an example. As a result, he sentenced you to three years in the state prison. When he pronounced sentence, the sky fell for you and your family.

Your experiences in prison have left you confused and frustrated. During those first few months of incarceration, you felt hopeless and alone. Your family, although upset and embarrassed, has stuck by you. The efforts of a young prison counselor and the support of your family have kept you going. Only six months remain on your sentence before you come up for parole. You have "kept your nose clean" with the prison staff and other inmates.

Last night a terrible incident occurred: Your eighteen-year-old cellmate, Sam, was brutally raped and beaten by four older inmates, who informed you that the same fate would be yours if you reported them. You remember only too well the whistles and the threats directed toward you during the first several days you were in the cellblock. You realize that your size and former athletic conditioning allowed you to establish a relative amount of independence in the prison; your cellmate, being smaller and weaker, had no such natural defense qualities. You also realize that if you report what they did to your friend, the four inmates are likely to make good their threat. Still, you cannot rid yourself of the rage and sickness you feel because of your friend's humiliation and helplessness. You know that he might be attacked again, yet you are also confronted with your own needs of survival and well-being.

The only employee you trust in the prison is a young counselor. Not having been at the prison very long, he has only a limited amount of influence with the prison administration. Nevertheless, he is enthusiastic and well intentioned. You cannot forget what happened to your cellmate, but with only six months before parole you are also thinking of your own welfare.

Questions for Discussion

1. What is the prison administration's moral obligation in protecting prison inmates from sexual abuse?
2. How could prison officials have done a better job to protect Sam from sexual assault?
3. Are there other ways to diminish the potential for sexual aggression in prison?

5

Home Sweet Home

Next Wednesday you will be walking out those front gates as a free man. This last time around cost you ten years. It was your third hitch. You have spent thirty of the last forty years of your life behind bars. Sixty-two years of life's ups and downs have softened your disposition. You have no excuses left; you feel that the time you got was coming to you. In fact, the last hitch was one you purposely set up.

When you were released the last time, it was a cold gray morning in February. There was no one on the outside waiting for you; your friends were all in prison. You had been divorced for over fifteen years and your former wife had remarried. Your parents were dead, and your two sisters had given up on you long ago. Besides, there were too many decisions to make in the free world. You were not used to all of that freedom; it was frightening. No one cared about you like they did inside the joint.

You got a job as a busboy in a restaurant, but the hustle and bustle was too much, and besides, no one wanted to make friends with an old ex-con. Finally you'd had all you could take, so you stole all the money from the cash register one night during a lull in business. You did not spend any of it but instead went home, had a beer, and waited. Once the restaurant manager realized you and the money were missing, it was not long before the police arrived at your apartment. In less than two hours, you were arrested. You refused an attorney and told the judge that you would keep committing crimes until he sent you back. He reluctantly sentenced you to ten years. You passed up parole each time it came around.

So here you are again. You have been measured for your new suit of street clothes and your $150 check for transitional expenses has been processed. The labor department representative has arranged for you to have a stock-clerk job in a small grocery store in a nearby town. Your social worker has also arranged for you to stay in a small apartment near the place where you will work. You remember your last prerelease counseling session with her and how she offered all the words of encouragement a young, energetic, and well-meaning counselor could muster. You just smiled and nodded. What good would it have done to burst her idealistic bubble? She could never understand how frightening the outside world had become for you. All of her friends lived in the free world; none of yours did.

You would like to make it on the outside if you could, but you know the odds are against you. And besides, it's just too lonely out there. You know you ought to feel happy about leaving prison, but the truth is, you are miserable about it. Although you want to make it on the outside, deep down inside you feel you are doomed before you start.

Questions for Discussion

1. Do departments of corrections have an ethical obligation to inmates to help them readjust to community life?
2. What kind of community programs might help with the transition of inmates from prison life to living in a free-world community?

6

A Legacy of Corruption

You are a young woman, born and reared in a rural area in the South. Your family was above average in relation to the working-class families in your town. Your father, a farmer, worked hard and saved his money. As a result he was able to provide you, your brother, two sisters, and your mother with a life of dignity and a sense of belonging—belonging to family, to town, and to country.

There was dignity, but no extras. Work was hard and income uncertain. Thriftiness was no mere virtue; it was a necessity. Your parents imbued you with the "American dream"—that hard work and education would make your life easier and more productive than theirs had been. By education, your parents meant high school and possibly some vocational training. After high school, you and one of your best friends decided to join the Air Force, enlisting for the full four years. You were assigned to a base in the North where you were able to learn a profession. Since your Air Force job was in personnel, you planned to seek work in a similar field when you were finally discharged.

When you returned to Smallberg and your family, you were ready to seek a career and a life of your own. Smallberg was home to you and you wanted to settle there, but there were no personnel jobs available. You felt that you would like to do something meaningful with your life. You wanted a job that would give you both security and a sense of accomplishment. You even considered reenlistment. Then you saw an advertisement:

> Correctional Officers needed at State Prison. Civil service position, fringe benefits, career opportunity. High school diploma required. Beginning salary $24,000. Apply at personnel office, main prison.

You couldn't believe your eyes! Twenty-four thousand dollars a year! Who could live on that? After several more weeks in a fruitless job search, you decided to apply for the position. You could live at home for awhile and at least the work would be meaningful.

Six weeks later you completed your basic correctional officers' training and with your fellow trainees you took and signed your oath of office as provided for in Section 26 of the state code:

> I do solemnly swear or affirm that I will faithfully and diligently perform all the duties required of me as an officer of the Department of Corrections and will observe and execute the laws, rules, and regulations passed and prescribed for the government thereof so far as the same concerns or pertains to my employment; that I will not ill treat or abuse any convict under my care, nor act contrary to the law, rules and regulations prescribed by legal authority, so help me God.

During the three years since you took the job at the state prison, you have observed worsening conditions. You have been promoted twice, but your annual gross pay is still only $26,500. The inmate population has increased 40 percent while there has only been a 10 percent increase in correctional officer positions. To make matters worse, the political and public mood has become increasingly negative. The education and recreation specialist positions have been eliminated, and three of the eight counselor positions have been frozen. No education programs, little if any organized recreation, more inmates, and fewer correctional officers have resulted in dismal working conditions.

Now, to increase your sense of frustration, you have learned that your captain and several other fellow officers are taking bribes from inmates in exchange for choice assignments. You mentioned to the captain that word has reached you with regard to the purchased assignments. Instead of being embarrassed or evasive the captain tells you, "These scumbags would sell their mothers for a dime and they deserve whatever happens to them." He then offers to assign you to the unit in charge of housing so that you can "get in on the action." There are even reports that several of the female officers are earning extra income by having sex with some of the better-connected inmates. Since you yourself have been propositioned twice during the last month, you have little doubt that the rumors are true.

Conflicting needs flood your consciousness. The last officer to complain about this particular captain was summarily dismissed and threatened with prosecution for possession of contraband that he claimed he was not even aware of. The captain's father is also a former warden of this prison, and his brother is the present business manager of the institution.

Needless to say, the situation has created a major crisis in your life. Your decision will be crucial because of its lasting implications for you. You value your personal integrity and you believe in the intrinsic value of your profession, yet you could use more money. In addition, there is the pragmatic necessity of your employment and your hope for advancement within the system—what there is left of it. You live in a beautiful, if depressed, economic area where few decent jobs exist. What should you do?

Questions for Discussion

1. In this case, should the correctional officer contact the prison superintendent or someone at the state level?
2. What kind of oversight or programs could effectively address corruption among corrections officers?

7

A Question of Policy

As a female correctional officer, you have been working at the same women's prison for fifteen years. The inmates call you Marge and respect you as being firm yet fair. You have made some mistakes during your career, but no one has ever questioned your intentions or integrity. Like anyone working in a prison, you have found that there were some inmates you liked more than others. However, it is rare for you to find an inmate with whom you cannot work at all. In fact, you are dedicated to the point that you will often spend some of your own time participating with the female inmates in recreation, arts and crafts, and other cell-block activities.

There is one inmate that you are particularly fond of. She is a young woman about nineteen years of age who is in on a drug offense. Lisa is a shy girl who comes from a broken home. She never had much of a family life; both of her parents had failed in previous marriages. Lisa's drug problems had started in high school when she got mixed up with the wrong crowd. She had felt accepted by the drug crowd, and besides, life had seemed easier to cope with while on drugs. Lisa was just beginning to use hard drugs when she got busted. Because she was with a friend who was selling large quantities of drugs, her bust resulted in a trial and a two-year sentence.

While in prison, Lisa has come to you on several occasions with personal problems. Being a first-time offender, she has found prison life very difficult to adjust to. You and she have become good friends in a mutually trusting relationship. On this particular day, however, your relationship is being tested.

Lisa has asked you to mail a personal letter to a close friend who lives in her home town. Since her friend is not a member of her family or her lawyer, his name is not on the approved mailing list. She knows your mailing the letter would be a violation of institutional policy but says it is very important to her that she contact her friend just this one time. You know that other correctional officers occasionally mail letters for inmates. You also realize that it would be quite easy for you to mail this particular letter. Still, it is a violation of policy.

If you do not mail the letter, your relationship with Lisa will more than likely deteriorate. If you do mail the letter, you may suffer unanticipated consequences. The decision is going to be a difficult one, and you are going to have to make it.

Questions for Discussion

1. Relationships of trust between inmates and correctional officers are not uncommon. How could such a small violation of prison policy create any problems?
2. What could the CO do to maintain the relationship and not violate the rules?
3. Is violating rules always an ethical transgression?

8

Confidentiality or Security?

You have been working as a counselor at the community correctional center for three years. You feel good about your job and the results you have achieved. No inmate or civilian has ever questioned Juan Lopez's ethics or integrity.

You are presently working on an especially interesting case. A young twenty-two-year-old second-time drug offender named Rafael has really been opening up to you and seems to be turning himself around in terms of his personal values and motivation. The trust between the two of you is apparent. In fact, just several days ago the superintendent commented on how much better your client seemed to be doing since you had taken him on your caseload. However, during the last counseling session your client disclosed something that could severely disrupt your relationship with him, and you are not sure what to do about it.

Halfway through your last session, in a moment of frustration, Rafael blurted the whole thing out. Apparently he and two other inmates had been planning an escape for some time. After Rafael became your client and began making progress, he had second thoughts about being involved in the escape. The other two inmates, however, threatened to implicate him if anything went wrong with their attempt. The escape attempt is planned for the following night. Rafael is distraught as to what he should do, and since you are his counselor, you are somewhat distraught also.

As a correctional counselor you are not only responsible for counseling inmates but have implicit security responsibilities as well. If the escape attempt is allowed to continue as planned, correctional officers, inmates, or both might be seriously injured or killed. If the plan is quashed, you will have failed to honor the confidentiality of your client, and Rafael will most probably suffer repercussions. Needless to say, your counseling relationship with him will also be severely damaged.

It seems you have to sacrifice either Rafael—and your counseling relationship with him—or the security of the correctional center. Confidentiality or security, which must it be? Can there be another way?

Questions for Discussion

1. Sometimes legal concerns conflict with client confidentiality. Although custody issues come first, what might the likely costs be to your therapeutic relationship with the inmate in question?
2. What other options are available?
3. Does Rafael have a right to ask you to remain quiet about the attempt?

9

Who's Running the Prison?

You came to the state correctional system with good credentials. You feel that your background—as an ex-military officer with fifteen years experience in high-level correctional management positions and a recently completed master's degree in criminal justice—qualifies you for almost any correctional-related position. You have a practical, no-nonsense attitude and feel quite comfortable in being appointed superintendent of the state penitentiary, which had been suffering from incompetent leadership and political intrigue.

The facility was in the state's most isolated corner, and the inmates there were either considered to have little potential for rehabilitation or were serving such long-term sentences that rehabilitation was of little immediate interest. In accepting the job as superintendent, you stated that your top priorities were to upgrade conditions in the prison, especially the physical plant, and to improve the quality of the correctional officer staff. Recently the two problems have become entwined in an unexpected way.

You had only been on the job for one week when the county commissioner for the district in which your institution is located came to see you. The commissioner, as you soon learned, was a political power in the county and could make conditions miserable for you if he wanted. It seems that his son-in-law needed a job, and he wanted you to find a place for him on your staff. One word led to another, and before you knew it you responded by stating, "Hell no! I won't hire anybody unless they are qualified."

The county commissioner left angrily, and a day later Senator Nester called. Senator Nester was on the state corrections committee and represented the district in which your institution was located. At the time he called you did not know that he was also on the appropriations committee. You learned later that if someone wanted a management job at the institution, he had to call Senator Nester in order to be hired. Senator Nester stated in his call to you that he just wanted to "get acquainted" and give you a little friendly advice. First, he indicated that you should make a serious effort to get along with all the local officials, and second, he recommended that you hire the county commissioner's son-in-law. You told the senator that you would look at the son-in-law's application when he submitted it, and if he was qualified, you would give him serious consideration, but beyond that you could make no promises.

Your review of the son-in-law's hastily submitted application revealed that he had a high school diploma, had been a police officer on a local force, and had held several other unrelated jobs, all of rather short duration. In short, he might be qualified for an entry-level correctional officer slot. However, his work record was spotty and the reason for his departure from the police department was unclear. Although no one was talking openly about it, there were some allegations circulating from certain members of the department of police brutality involving the son-in-law. Since you did not want an unqualified and questionable political hack in your organization, you placed his application in "file 13."

After a week Senator Nester's office called "on behalf of a constituent" and inquired about the son-in-law's application. Your personnel officer told the senator's office that a letter had been sent to the applicant thanking him for his application, but informing him that applications were competitive and, unfortunately, he had not been selected.

Later in the day Senator Nester called back in person; he was enraged. "Why wasn't I informed of your decision? I've done a hell of a lot for this correctional system and have a right to expect the courtesy of a reply. I never had this problem before." Nester was clearly threatening when he said, "You may find that these upcoming hearings will question your practices in dealing with the legislature, and I'll have some questions about your personnel policies, too." You finally told Senator Nester that you were running the institution, and until you were replaced you would continue to hire people based on merit.

Two months later at budget hearings in the legislature, you found out Senator Nester was a man of his word. Because of his influence, a new car for the prison superintendent was stricken, slots for eighteen new correctional officers were also stricken, and to make matters worse, the committee voted to nullify the badly needed pay raises that had been budgeted for all the prison employees.

The senator's message has come through to you loud and clear. You realize that the two of you will have to reach some sort of working agreement, unless you can marshal enough support from other more friendly legislators, which at present does not seem likely. How should you approach Senator Nester? How can you maintain your standards and at the same time appease him? Should you give and take a little, should you look for a new job, or should you do both? You are not a quitter; you would prefer to work with Senator Nester, but you keep asking yourself how.

Questions for Discussion

1. What are some ways a powerful senator can corrupt a correctional facility located in his district?
2. Is there anything the prison superintendent can do to remedy the situation?

10

Sexual Harassment

What a mess! You let out a deep sigh as you hang up the telephone. Sitting at your desk staring out the window, you listen to the rain and try to slowly collect your thoughts.

Maria Diaz has just called you in tears. Three years ago she was part of your caseload. This time around she is assigned to Ned, your office supervisor. When Maria was originally assigned to you for case supervision, she had been convicted of drug possession and prostitution. You remember her well: an attractive sixteen-year-old Latina with a one-year-old daughter, a drug addiction, a police record, and very little education.

You worked with her for two years and watched her gradually dig her way out of the hole in which she had found herself and build a life with some hope. She earned a GED degree, and with the help and support of a caring grandmother she learned how to become a mother herself. When she finished her term of probation, she found a job in an upscale department store selling cosmetics and women's fashions. You felt her chances to make it were excellent. She seemed to have improved her sense of self-esteem and had dreams of one day owning and operating her own fashion boutique.

Apparently something has happened in the year following her release from probation that could jeopardize Maria's success. Relapses happen. You have been in the business for fifteen years and it still disappoints you when someone doesn't make it. What makes Maria's current situation even more frustrating is that it involves Ned, your supervisor.

Ned is white, 46 years old, and divorced. Maria has just tearfully informed you that Ned has grown increasingly aggressive over the last three months, trying to force her into a sexual relationship with him. Apparently he is offering her unsupervised probation in exchange for sexual favors and threatening her with revocation if she refuses his advances. You recall Maria's words, "He told me that since I once was a prostitute, it shouldn't be a big deal. He even offered me money if I was good enough." You get a sick feeling in your stomach when you recall what she said.

You have heard rumors about Ned. This probably isn't the first time he has done something like this. You have never seen any proof of the rumors, so you never accepted them as being true. Besides, Ned has always been good to you. Now you find yourself feeling angry and foolish. This time you are going to have to act. You gave Maria all the reassurance you could and promised to get back to her.

You have to respond to this problem, but how? You consider calling Tom Johnson, the regional supervisor, but are uncertain about this course of action since he and Ned are good friends. In fact, they play golf together every week. You also realize that getting caught in the middle of this problem can harm your own career. After all, you do have a wife and children. Besides, Maria hasn't exactly been a model of virtue in the past. She has brought a lot of this trouble on herself. Still, it isn't right for Ned to abuse his power over a client. He's white, she's Hispanic and a woman, and you are caught right in the middle of a very uncomfortable situation.

Questions for Discussion

1. While sexual harassment is both illegal and unethical, how is Ned using his position to intimidate the probationer in question?
2. What can you do about this situation?
3. What are some safeguards that might diminish the potential for such problems?

11

Prisons for Profit

The corporate lobbyist was convincing. If the state statutes were changed, many of the day-to-day problems of coping with an ever expanding state correctional system could be given to someone else to manage. The responsibility for correcting its offenders would always remain with the state, but a part of the day-to-day management of the system could be given to the private sector by contract. Private police forces have been around for a long time—why not private corrections?

Your legislature had little trouble crafting and passing the enabling legislation. Other states, Canada, and Australia were using the idea, the pros were economic and the cons were philosophical; in such a game, the pros will win every time. At least, that's what the proponents of privatization argued.

The drawing of the contract presents the usual problem. The state has a standard services contract with a thirty-day termination clause on a one-year contract, and the corporation has a standard contract with a one-year termination clause on a five-year contract. The corporation argues that this is the only way they can recoup their multimillion-dollar capital investment and give new programs a fair chance to work. Some of the more troubling aspects of the contract include the use of deadly force, inmate discipline, and escape; the rest is more easily worked out.

The prison will be built and managed according to American Correctional Association (ACA) standards. The building will be leased by the state from the corporation for five years, and management may be terminated for cause with thirty days notice plus time for appeal. The department of corrections would exercise full authority to assign, reassign and approve classification of inmates at the private facility. The custodial force would be selected and trained by ACA standards. The state department of corrections would have the authority to approve those selected for the top managerial position at each private institution. Most important to the corporation, the state would pay a flat rate for inmate services, i.e., food, housing and medicine based on a minimum 90 percent of capacity.

Further, the state agreed not to exceed the rated capacity. This provided a guaranteed income for the corporation while assuring that the state would keep their private institutions full, even if the state institutions were not. The theory is that the state institutions are less efficient, more expensive to operate, and in more demand for the most difficult and long-term inmates. Regarding the 10 percent of capacity not guaranteed in the contract, there were always that many in transit and in the hospital.

Major medical care continued to be a big line item in the department budget, and the corporation will not be responsible for hospital care, only dispensary-type services for minor ailments, cuts, and bruises. Once admitted to the hospital, the inmate is in the immediate custody and care of the state.

With the enabling legislation in place, your department signed the contract with some misgivings. Three 250-bed units, two minimum security and one medium security, were the first to be built. Transition from ground breaking to full operations status in less than a year was the goal. The state could never do that. So far so good.

The initial stages of the relationship between the department and the private corporation are good. The corporation hired a retired member of your staff to manage the project. The legislature's budget office has figured out that at $20 per day per inmate paid to the corporation, the state will be saving about $1,100 per inmate housed in these facilities per year including the lease of the facility.

After the first year, the honeymoon was over. An improving local economy has caused the corporation to look elsewhere for a labor pool. Retired correctional officers are finding jobs in the new auto plant, and new college graduates are more attracted to government service because of better benefits. You had always suspected that reducing employee benefits would, in the end, be a primary way the private corporation would try to make money.

At breakfast your deputy for institutions called. "Commissioner, I hate to start your day off this way, but we had an escape at Corporate Unit A last night. Apparently the inmate walked right out of the institution with a work crew, and they have no leads on his whereabouts. His sister, his only relative, lives in Canada. No telling where we will find him."

"What is he in for? Is he dangerous?" you quickly ask.

"We do not think he is dangerous, he is in for forgery and auto theft. His record shows multiple counts on each. Apparently he would take a car on a demonstration ride, hightail it to some place he had supplies, forge a title, then sell it before the data got into the NCIC. Sometimes he would have a stolen license plate and sometimes he would not. Some of the inmates said he worked in a print shop for a while. My guess is that he is long gone."

"I hate to see this happen this soon in the new program. How about having internal affairs check this out and see if the corporation's security procedures are being followed. Also, have them look at the background of the officers on duty at the time of the escape."

"Good idea," says your deputy. "You can't tell who they are hiring with the job market improving so much on the outside. I have even heard their recent hires referred to as McGuards."

Internal affairs verified what you suspected, that the facility was working short-handed that night because one of the correctional officers assigned to check passes at the gate had resigned on short notice and a replacement had not been found. The security chief will be admonished.

The other problems that came up were mostly due to posturing, contract interpretation, and the corporation's desire not to spend a nickel unless they had to. But the clincher finally came three months later when the escapee was apprehended by the Royal Canadian Mounted Police around the Hudson Bay area in Canada after he sold a four-wheel drive truck that had been stolen in the United States. Canadian officials would happily agree to extradition because he was a U.S. citizen, but the resulting problem has developed into a major disagreement with the corporation—namely, who is going to pick up the prisoner, and who is going to pay the expenses? It could easily cost over $5,000 in travel when the tab is paid, plus the human-resources loss of a badly needed correctional officer who would be drawing overtime, of course. You pour yourself another cup of coffee and lean back in your chair, mulling over the situation. You wonder if private corrections means less money or more headaches, or maybe both.

Questions for Discussion

1. What are the ethical implications of "prisons for profit?"
2. How can a private prison be effective and still make a profit?
3. What sort of oversight should exist to regulate such privatization programs?

12

Death Row Dilemma

Warden Ellis Thompson had overseen four executions during his tenure at the state prison. Each of them proved to be a difficult challenge in their own unique way. Now he was two weeks away from overseeing the execution of Ronnie Simpkins, a 28-year-old black man accused of raping and murdering a young mother of two, who happened to be white. With a single eye witness who happened to be a two-time loser and several pieces of questionable circumstantial evidence, the jury had taken only 45 minutes to reach a guilty verdict. Having grown up in a rural community, Ellis enjoyed the benefits of a close-knit community. Still, 45 minutes to reach a guilty verdict based upon the evidence he reviewed begs the question of whether justice was served—especially for anyone who knew Ronnie Simpkins.

Assistant Warden Gus Hall plopped down on the sofa as Ellis chewed on his third extra-strength Tums.

"You got another gut-ache?" Pouring a glass of water, the warden offered Gus a wry smile.

"At least these Tums taste better than that bottle of Maalox I polished off last night."

Gus folded his hands over his ample belly. "Well, you might want to keep that bottle of Tums handy. I just got off the phone with Mr. and Mrs. Simpkins. You know his father's a pastor?"

"Yeah, I know," Ellis replied as he took a swallow of water.

"Well," Gus continued, "They are of the opinion that Chaplain Decker is racially insensitive to their son."

Rubbing his chin, Ellis stared at the gathering clouds outside his office window. "I've heard the chaplain's upset several of the inmates with his fire-and-brimstone approach to things."

"Then there's the fact that he's the governor's brother-in-law to take into consideration," Gus replied.

Ellis turned his gaze back to his assistant warden and smiled. "Then there's that."

Gus patted his stomach and grinned. "Here we are in tight budget times, having to make cuts even though we are short a dozen correctional officers, and a new position has been added to the roster which happens to be a chaplain slot. Guess it's a miracle."

"Nothing short of a miracle," Ellis replied, drumming his fingers on the desk-top.

"For us or him, Warden? Especially since he got fired from his last two positions."

"Gus, I'll let you make that call," Ellis responded, sticking a toothpick in his mouth. "It's bad enough that Ronnie Simpkins is facing execution, but he and his family having to deal with Chaplain Decker just adds to their burden. Besides, Simpkins isn't like the others."

Gus lowered his eyes. "Yeah, I also took a close look at Simpkins's case and background. Good family. No trouble with the law. Great work record. And an impressive list of character witnesses."

Ellis leaned forward. "Gus, I don't believe Simpkins is guilty. It doesn't make sense. The evidence doesn't support his conviction. He's broken up fights in the cell house—put himself at risk more than once to protect other inmates. And he knows a hell of a lot more about the Bible than Decker does."

"I agree that Simpkins is a good man, one of the best I've come across in this place—inmate or free world. But you and me ain't the jury or the judge. Not our job," Gus interjected.

Ellis gripped the edge of his desk. "Right's right and wrong's wrong. And Simpkins has always maintained his innocence."

Gus clasped his hands together. "He's never seemed bitter."

Ellis took another swallow of water. "That's the unsettling part. He's calm. He has a deep faith."

"Said he got it from his daddy," the assistant warden replied.

Ellis returned his gaze to the window. "The other executions were hard enough, but at least it was clear that they were guilty. But this time . . ."

Gus got to his feet. "Rain's coming in. What you want me to tell Simpkins's parents?"

"Tell them I'll remove Decker from his death row Chaplain duties—and give our apologies for their distress."

Gus shrugged. "The Governor won't be happy."

Ellis flipped the toothpick in the trash can. "Won't matter that much. It's too close to next election and he's not the pardoning kind. I may not be able to make the big wrong right, but maybe we can give Mr. Simpkins and his family a little peace and dignity. I could use a little myself about now."

Questions for Discussion

1. How do you think you might feel if you were the warden overseeing an execution? What if you were overseeing the execution of someone you felt was innocent?

2. How can politics play a role in corrections? What would you do as warden if the governor offered you his brother-in-law as a staff member? What are some ethical issues in terms of personnel and staffing procedures?
3. What are some ways states who execute inmates for capital crimes can make sure they don't execute an innocent person?

13

Correctional Counseling?

As a shift sergeant in the County Corrections Complex, you try to keep a close eye on your officers and the inmates. The fact that the facility holds both men and women inmates creates even more challenges. You have been concerned about a first-year correctional officer who seems to spend a little too much time around a particular female inmate.

Pouring yourself another cup of coffee, you think about your scheduled meeting with Lieutenant Alvarez, the shift supervisor. You've seen it before—male officer hooks up with female inmate, or female officer hooks up with male inmate and, in one high profile case six years ago, tries to help him escape. That situation hit the front page and even got a brief mention on national news. Even though the inmate was captured and the female officer arrested, the bad publicity cost the sheriff his job in the following election. Many of the correctional officers, especially the young ones, don't seem to pay attention to the consequences for such behavior. It's a part of their orientation. Fraternization with inmates is a felony. They should know better.

"Have a seat, Gene. What's on your mind?"

You looked at your lieutenant. "We got a potential problem with one of our new officers, Jimmy Atwater. He's hanging around one of the female inmates a little too much for my liking."

The lieutenant folded his hands on the desk. "Who is she?"

"Velma Martin," you replied.

Lieutenant Alvarez smiled. "She is a looker. No doubt about that. Word is that she gets quite a few notes slipped to her from some of the male inmates."

"She is a pretty woman," you replied. "Her rap sheet indicates she has been well paid for her looks on more than one occasion. Some of those fellows might well have been her customers."

"Have you talked with Atwater?" the lieutenant responded, looking at his watch.

"Yes sir, I did. Atwater denied there was a problem. Said he took a correctional counseling course at the community college and was counseling her about her problems."

"I didn't realize a community college course qualified you to be a counselor," Lieutenant Alvarez chuckled. "Seems our young Mr. Atwater thinks he's Sigmund Freud."

You crossed your arms over your chest. "Don't know about that, sir, but Atwater is no match for Ms. Martin. I think he's headed for trouble."

Lieutenant Alvarez looked at his watch again. "That may be, but you have warned him. He's a grown man. If he gets in trouble, it will be his own fault. Just keep an eye on him and Miss Velma."

You looked at Sergeant Alvarez, who asked, "Anything else, Gene? I got to take the sheriff to some rubber-chicken Kiwanis meeting. Just keep an eye on the wanna-be counselor."

"Nothing else, sir," you replied. "Will do."

Walking through the recreation yard, you spotted Atwater talking with Velma Martin in a private corner. You could hear her laugh at something the officer said as he walked by. Atwater had bordered on being disrespectful to you during your last encounter. You had done your duty and reported the situation to the lieutenant. You were tempted to let Atwater "hang himself." Velma Martin would give him plenty of rope. Still, you hated to see the young man ruin his life. You could give Atwater a "tough love" talk. Maybe that would shake him up enough to see the error of his ways, or maybe it wouldn't.

QUESTIONS FOR DISCUSSION

1. Your have tried to warn the young correctional officer about the consequences of fraternizing with the female inmate in question, and Officer Atwater did receive training about the dangers as well. Have you done enough?
2. Can professionals like Officer Atwater assume too much authority concerning a course they might take like "correctional counseling"? Does the teacher or instructor have a responsibility to discuss the limits and professional requirements to do counseling?
3. Did Lieutenant Alvarez demonstrate any degree of sexism in discussing the situation with you?

Section IV

ETHICS AND JUVENILE JUSTICE

The origin and legacy of the juvenile justice system lie in the *parens patriae* concept—the state figuratively takes the place of the parent in family and juvenile courts. The goal of the court system is to do what is best for the juvenile, a very different goal than that of the adult system. Each of the areas addressed in the first three sections of this casebook must be revisited in addressing juvenile offenders. How should we enforce the laws against juveniles? What rights do juveniles possess when accused of a crime? How should juveniles be punished? Does a juvenile ever belong in a correctional facility that houses adults?

One of the first questions to consider in the realm of juvenile justice is moral and legal culpability. Do juveniles have the same culpability as adults? While we accept the obvious reality that a four-year-old does not have the moral or legal culpability of a 21-year-old, there is no clear answer to that question in the intervening years. What level of intellectual development is necessary to understand murder? Lionel Tate killed a neighborhood girl when he was 12, imitating a wrestling move he had seen on television. Should his age excuse his actions to any degree? He was sentenced to life without parole, although after serving three years his conviction was overturned and he agreed to a plea agreement. Can a 12-year-old form the *mens rea* that creates legal culpability for first-degree murder? What about moral culpability? If not, what about a 13-year-old, 14-year-old, or 16-year-old? When can someone be considered an adult in their reasoning ability?

Today people are less likely to agree that juveniles should be dealt with differently, and thousands of juveniles are referred to the adult court. Depending on the state, referral may be mandatory or permissive for certain crimes and certain ages. When a juvenile is referred to an adult court from a juvenile court, the judge typically considers age, mental competency, seriousness of crime, dangerousness, and "the interests of justice." There were 7,560 children under 18 in jails for adults in 2010 either awaiting trial, serving a misdemeanor sentence, or being adjudicated in the juvenile system but in a locale that had no juvenile lockups (Minton, 2011). Most of them had been referred to adult courts and will be prosecuted and serve time with adults. Note that not all, or even most, of the juveniles who are referred to adult courts commit violent acts; many are property offenders. If juveniles are not allowed to make the decision to drive, buy alcohol, or smoke cigarettes because we do not believe they can make responsible decisions about the use of these products, why do we hold them responsible for criminal action?

If juveniles are less culpable than adults, what should we do with them? Detention centers for juveniles bear all the same indices of adult prisons and may be no less damaging. In such facilities, juveniles are removed from their families and subjected to close residency with other juvenile delinquents—if prisons are called schools of crime, certainly it can be argued that juvenile incarceration facilities are even more so. Are professionals who work with juveniles more likely to pursue rehabilitative goals, or do they (like their counterparts in adult institutions) experience burnout and frustration? When juveniles have committed serious crimes, what should happen when they turn 21? Should they be transferred to an adult prison or released?

One of the hallmarks of the juvenile court is that it handles issues of delinquency, status offenses, and family custody issues as part of its mandate. Thus, the same court might rule on a case where a juvenile committed a violent crime and a case where a juvenile has been neglected and/or abused. The rationale of the juvenile justice system is that all juveniles need care and supervision. If parents do not provide care and supervision, the state must do so. The state must step in and perform the "parental" function, whether the juvenile has committed an act that could be a crime (delinquency), has committed an act that is not a crime if committed by an adult (status offense), or is simply showing signs of neglect or abuse (in which case the child becomes a ward of the state).

There has been a widespread belief that juvenile crime is growing. This belief no doubt has spurred the increase in the number of juveniles referred to adult courts. Contrary to belief, however, the juvenile arrest rate was lower in 2008 than it was in 1980. The juvenile arrest rate for all offenses was at its highest level in 1996 and dropped by 33% by 2008, when for ages 10–17 there were 6,318 arrests for every 100,000 youths (OJJDP, 2009).

Crime has always been called a "young man's game," and that continues to be the case. It could also be the case, however, that we are more likely to utilize formal processing for acts that, in days past, would have been handled informally. Today most schools have a "zero tolerance" policy, and even the most minor incidents of fighting or misbehavior on the school grounds result in police being called. Some schools have police officers permanently assigned to the school, and no doubt they are more likely to use formal alternatives.

In the past, because of the different philosophy of the juvenile court and the idea that it served in the best interest of the child, hearings tended to be much more informal than those in adult criminal courts. In the 1960s and 1970s a series of Supreme Court cases identified and clarified due process rights that juveniles facing prosecution deserved. Whether or not the juvenile justice system was making decisions "in the best interest" of the child, the Supreme Court made it clear that there must be certain protections of due process, for the same reason that they exist in adult court. In *Kent v. United States*, 383 U.S. 541 (1966), the Court held that before a judge could waive a juvenile over to adult court, there must be a hearing to determine if the juvenile was competent. In the case *In re Gault*, 387 U.S. 1 (1967), a 15-year-old was sentenced to the State Industrial School until the age of 21 for an obscene phone call. Note that the act would have only received at most a misdemeanor jail sentence if committed by an adult. The Court held that Gault was deprived of due process rights because he was not notified of the charges against him, he wasn't given counsel, he had no privilege against self-incrimination, no witnesses were sworn, no transcript was made, and his parents weren't notified. The Court made it clear that due process rights must be accorded juveniles facing punitive sanctions.

Since then, there have been other cases that have clarified the due process rights necessary in the prosecution of juveniles. The Supreme Court has also ruled that it was unconstitutionally cruel and unusual to execute juveniles. First, in *Thompson v. Oklahoma*, 487 U.S. 815 (1988), the Court ruled that it was a violation of the Eighth Amendment to execute an offender who committed his offense before his sixteenth birthday. That left the age range of 16–18 in doubt. In a subsequent case, the Court ruled that a juvenile offender who committed his crime before his eighteenth birthday could not be executed (*Roper v. Simmons*, No. 03-633, decided March 2005). Before this case, the United States alone of all Western countries allowed for the execution of those who committed their crime as young as seventeen years of age. The execution of juveniles violates the United Nations Convention on the Rights of the Child; however, the United States has never adopted it. In *Roper*, the Court cited the "evolving standards of decency" argument and overturned prior court decisions that allowed juvenile executions.

Another issue is how juveniles should be interrogated. Most states have special procedural protections for juveniles that require the presence of their parents and/or counsel. The argument is that juveniles are especially vulnerable to implicit or explicit coercion. Some states also require video recording of the confessions of juveniles. These protections are no doubt necessary—for example, the infamous "Central Park Jogger" case that occurred in New York City when a young woman was brutally attacked and raped while running in Central Park. Several youths were arrested for the offense, confessed, and received prison sentences.

Years later, another man confessed, and DNA evidence supported his admission that he was the only one involved in the attack. The youths—who later professed their innocence and stated that police had threatened them if they did not confess—were exonerated, but not before they spent many years in prison. The major arguments against juveniles being interrogated without parents present is that they do not understand their rights, they are easily intimidated and cowed by adult authority, and they are easily manipulated and coerced. This is not to say that police officers *intend* to manipulate, intimidate, or coerce juveniles, but it can happen.

Of course we also know that some juveniles are violent, some have entrenched criminal tendencies, and some are more knowledgeable about the criminal justice system than many adults. Mere youthfulness cannot be a "pass" to commit any type of crime and get away with it. Note, too, that juvenile crime ranges in severity from school shooting cases like the Columbine incident to knocking over mailboxes for "kicks." Children are also used in the drug trade because of a belief that they will encounter less severe punishments than would adults in similar circumstances. If a parent has their 15-year-old son delivering drugs for them, what would you do with the 15-year-old—is he as guilty as a 15-year-old who has law-abiding parents but becomes involved in criminal drug dealing on his own?

In summary, the types of ethical issues that revolve around juvenile offenders come in the form of major societal issues—whether to prosecute juveniles in adult courts, and whether to incarcerate them in adult prisons. There are also individual dilemmas that judges face when trying to decide what is in the best interest of the child and society.

Suggestions for Further Reading

Chambliss, W. (2011). *Juvenile crime and justice: Key issues in crime and punishment*. Thousand Oaks, CA: Sage.

Chesney-Lind, M., & Shelden, R. (2003). *Girls, delinquency and juvenile justice*. Belmont, CA: Wadsworth.

Del Carmen, R., & Trulson, C. (2005). *Juvenile justice: The system, process and law*. Belmont, CA: Wadsworth.

Humes, E. (1997). *No matter how loud I shout: A year in the life of juvenile court*. New York: Simon and Schuster.

Krisberg, B. (2004). *Juvenile justice: Redeeming our children*. Thousand Oaks, CA: Sage.

Kupchik, A. (2006). *Judging juveniles: Prosecuting adolescents in adult and juvenile court*. New York: New York University Press.

Mays, G. L., & Winfree, L. T. (2006). *Juvenile justice* (2nd ed.). Long Grove, IL: Waveland Press.

Minton, T. (2011). *Jail inmates at midyear 2010*. Washington, DC: U.S. Department of Justice, Bureau of Justice Statistics.

Newman, K. (2005). *Rampage: The social roots of school shootings*. New York: Basic Books.

Office of Juvenile Justice and Delinquency Prevention. (2009). *Statistical briefing book*. Retrieved from http://www.ojjdp.gov/ojstatbb/crime/JAR_Display.asp?ID=qa05200

Parry, D. (2004). *Essential readings in juvenile justice*. Upper Saddle River, NJ: Prentice-Hall.

Platt, A. (1977). *The child savers: The invention of delinquency*. Chicago: University of Chicago Press.

Scott, E., & Steinberg, L. (2010). *Rethinking juvenile justice*. Cambridge, MA: Harvard University Press.

Shelden, R. G. (2006). *Delinquency and juvenile justice in American society*. Long Grove, IL: Waveland Press.

Whitehead, J. (2003). *Juvenile justice*. Cincinnati, OH: Anderson.

1

The Teacher, the Delinquent, and the Gang

Schools have certainly changed since you last taught in the classroom. It used to be short hair, no jeans, no slacks, and no fun! One of the reasons students looked forward to college was that they could do and dress as they pleased. But now, high schools are becoming very similar to college in many respects. Such traditions as study hall and home room are beginning to disappear. Many high schools allow students much more flexibility in choosing the courses they take, which is a pleasant change from the school system you recall. You remember well how much you hated the conformity. Not only are students now allowed more freedom in choosing courses, but teachers are also allowed more freedom in experimenting with different teaching methods. As a fifty-six-year-old teacher with a newly earned master of education degree, who hasn't taught in more than twenty years, you have a number of ideas on how to improve the quality and interest of classroom instruction. Yet, you realize a twenty-five-year absence is a long time, and you know that things have changed since you stopped teaching to raise a family. Your husband, a retired city engineer, cautioned you not to expect too much too soon; nevertheless, you remained optimistic about the possibilities regarding innovating educational techniques.

You found out quickly that some of the changes in contemporary high schools might not have been for the better. When you taught high school, the teacher was considered "boss" and his or her word was usually law. For those few students who did not accept it, the threat of detention or possible expulsion helped to convince them. Now, however, student discipline seems to be growing worse, if it exists at all. In fact, your school principal, who believes in strict discipline, has been brought to court twice for being too punitive. Because the judge in your community also believes in strict discipline, the principal won both cases. However, student behavior has continued to become more aggressive in your high school, as demonstrated by several recent physical assaults on teachers. And to make matters worse, several groups of students have emerged that are beginning to look more and more like gangs.

There appear to be three primary neophyte gangs vying for attention. The first, The Rosewood Brothers, was apparently inspired by a recent popular film and includes about a dozen young African-American males ranging in age from fourteen to eighteen. The second, the Border Runners, is comprised primarily of young Mexican-American males whose members number about a dozen and seem to be concentrated in the fifteen- to sixteen-year-old age range. A third smaller group, the Invisible Empire, is made up of five or six underachieving white male students with shaven heads who look like skinhead "wannabes." Of course, several girls also affiliate with each gang. Other than several fist fights and petty acts of vandalism, there have been no major confrontations. However, recently several members of the Invisible Empire have boasted of getting their hands on two AK-47s. Mr. Smith, the principal of your school, seems a little nervous but hopes that several key graduations will take away the leadership of the gangs in question. You aren't so sure.

Against this backdrop, you are currently faced with a significant discipline problem in one of your own classes. A fifteen-year-old female student has consistently refused to cooperate with you regarding course assignments and behavior in the classroom. She hangs around the Border Runners. At times she is belligerent, and at other times she simply ignores you. And every so often—just often enough to give you a faint sense of hope—she contributes something creative and positive to a class discussion. Unfortunately, just as quickly she reverts to a rebellious act. Needless to say, such behavior also encourages other members of the class to be disruptive. In addition, several members of the Border Runners who are also in your class occasionally encourage her to be disruptive.

This particular student has been in trouble with the police since she was ten years old for truancy, occasional shoplifting, and minor vandalism. You have heard that the juvenile court judge has indicated that one more incident will send her to training school for a long stint. The principal has agreed to have her expelled from school; expulsion would probably result in her being sent to training school.

You are uncertain as to what course of action to take. You would hate to see the student sent to training school, but you doubt other disciplinary measures would do any good. On the other hand, you can accomplish very little in class as long as she continues to misbehave. You have tried to contact her parents, but they do not respond to your personal notes or your phone calls. Her affiliation with the Border Runners, as well as the larger issue of the emergence of the gangs themselves, concerns you. Something needs to be done, but what?

Questions for Discussion

1. What are your ethical responsibilities as a teacher? As a citizen?
2. What are some ways in which you could work proactively with local law enforcement officials to address emerging problems confronting some of your students?
3. How can kids be taught to be more ethical, which includes acting responsibly at school?

2

A Family of Offenders

Jake is thirteen years old, a little small for his age, yet wise in the ways of the world and as tough as a marine drill sergeant. Jake's usual racket is "protection." For a portion of the other sixth-graders' lunch money, Jake will guarantee that they will not be harassed by the playground bullies, of whom Jake is the most likely hazard.

Since being assigned as a juvenile aftercare worker in the county youth court, you have already seen Jake on several occasions and have heard many stories about his family, which your counterpart in the adult court calls "a breeding ground for felons." It is well known that six of Jake's eight brothers and sisters have served jail sentences, and two brothers are presently in the state penitentiary. Sam, the oldest, is twenty-two years old and is serving eight years for armed robbery. Richard, age nineteen, is serving twenty years for kidnapping and attempted rape of a high school girl who was walking home from school. Jake's two sisters, age seventeen and eighteen, have long records of shoplifting. The older one was involved in a killing at a local lounge and may be indicted at the next grand jury term.

If Jake's early conduct is any indication, he will deserve the description of "felon" as soon as the youth court statutes allow. Jake was not thought to be a proper candidate for a foster home or a group home, so he was committed to the state juvenile training schools on three occasions. His commitment did not seem to have any effect on his subsequent conduct, except that his grades improved after each period.

You have decided to visit Jake's home to talk to his mother. The specific reason for the visit is that he has been associating with a group of four older boys (two of whom are believed to be his brothers) who are thought to be involved in a series of local "lovers' lane" robberies. The robbers always leave the scene on foot. On one occasion, a fourth member of the band, acting as a lookout, ran up to the three who were committing the robbery to warn them of an approaching car. Although identification was incomplete, a composite sketch created a strong implication that Jake was the lookout. The rest of the gang had worn stocking masks.

Jake's family lives in a three-room flat in the ghetto. Mattresses criss-cross the floor of the common bedroom, and there is a new color television—"a gift from a friend," his mother said—in the living room and kitchen combination. The third room appeared to be the mother's private bedroom.

The apartment was dirty, and the furniture in the main room gave the feeling of a waiting room rather than a family-centered area. You gathered that mama was probably in business for herself, and that it was up to the three children who remained at home to take care of themselves. You doubted that your talk with Jake's mother would produce anything except evasiveness and hostility.

Jake's mother, obviously just out of bed for your 1:00 PM appointment, was belligerent and denied any possibility that Jake could be in any trouble, or even heading for trouble. She finally admitted that Jake had been in trouble "once or twice" and then became abusive, blaming the police for her son's trouble. She asked you unceremoniously to "get out and don't come back."

About a month later, Jake and his brothers were arrested by a police undercover team posing as a lovers' lane couple. The juvenile court waived jurisdiction, and Jake was sent to adult court. Although the court-appointed defense attorney attempted to have Jake tried separately, he and his brothers were tried together, and all were sentenced to a term in the state prison for adult males.

Because of his youth, Jake's sentence was suspended. You are asked by the adult probation supervisor to help with Jake's supervision (both adult and juvenile probation functions are integrated under the same authority in your state). Although Jake is legally bound to serve an adult sentence and is responsible to the adult court, you may hold the key to his eventual rehabilitation. On the other hand, there may be no such key. You want to salvage Jake from a career of crime, but the "odds" do not look good. Is there anything you can possibly do, or should you just write Jake off?

Questions for Discussion

1. In this case, as a product of a "criminal" environment, Jake is quickly becoming just another criminal justice statistic. Could he be removed from this environment? Where could he be sent? What would be the consequences of such action on Jake and his family? Are there other alternatives?
2. Is it ethical to threaten the mother with jail, even though you know the system probably can't do anything to her?
3. Is it ethical to convince the judge that Jake should spend his probation in the juvenile detention facility so you don't have to deal with him?

4. In a broader sense, do social institutions such as the educational system and human service agencies bear any ethical responsibilities to try to prevent youths such as Jake from becoming full-blown criminals? What are some ways in which such institutions could assess and respond to youths like Jake in order to increase their chances for more positive and law-abiding outcomes?

3

A Choice of Punishments

Pat is a seventeen-year-old high school junior with nothing to do during the summer. No job, no summer school, no camps, nothing. For some reason, public summer programs for youths like Pat are very scarce or nonexistent. It is the Fourth of July, hot, and Pat is looking for some diversion. Pat's friend, Al Schultz, comes by in his antique pick-up truck that he has spent the last six months rebuilding, and he invites Pat to a party that he will be attending at a friend's apartment in the project. The friend's parents are away for the day.

Although Al is a few months older than Pat and dropped out of high school, he always seems to have money—not much, but some. Al tells Pat that he has to go by the grocery store to pick up a case of beer and also get some gas. Pat is impressed until Al drives up to a two-pump Quick Stop, parks beside a car that is filling up so he cannot be seen by the cashier, fills up, then jumps in the truck and drives off. The attendant made the mistake of letting the pump run without being able to see the vehicle being filled up. Pat is not too happy with this, but it was so slick, the way he edged up to the pumps behind the other automobile, that there seems to be little danger of getting caught.

Next, Al drives to a grocery store for beer. He parks at the corner of the building, out of sight of the cashiers in the store, and asks Pat to watch the truck because he wants to leave the motor running. "Sometimes it is hard to start when it is hot," explains Al. Pat waits patiently, and in a few minutes Al comes out the door of the grocery with a case of beer and drives off. Apparently, Al legitimately purchased a case of beer and Pat will be able to share it with him at the party. "Good friend, old Al," Pat mutters to himself.

The next day Pat's mother tells him there is a police officer at the door with a warrant for his arrest. Not only did the Quick Stop clerk get a description and partial license plate number, but the manager of the grocery store followed Al and got the full tag number as well as a description of the occupants of the truck. Al has already been arrested and identified Pat as his companion. In their state, accessories to misdemeanors are treated as principals, and Pat is one. Pat tells the police officers he was only a passenger. Yes, he helped drink the beer. All right, he rode in a truck with gas he knew was stolen, and he sat in the car when Al left it running to go get the beer, but he did not do anything illegal himself—and he had no knowledge that the beer had been stolen.

After his conversation with the investigating officers, he is taken to the police station, booked for two counts of petty larceny, and released to his mother's custody. He is to appear in city court to answer to the charges a week from Monday at 9:00 AM.

Pat finally talks to Al, who apologizes for implicating him but says, "I had no choice." Al suggests that Pat and he leave the state since the police will not come after them in another state just for a misdemeanor. Pat thinks about it, but he is in enough trouble as it is, and running away would not help anything. Pat had been into some vandalism once before and a couple of incidents of shoplifting, and nothing had happened other than he had to make restitution, so he decides to go to court and take his chances.

Judge Ward, the city judge, has recently been elected to his post. He is a retired FBI agent who ran on a platform of "getting tough on crime." Judge Ward has been said to not have allowed the phrase, "not guilty," to pass his lips since elected. Hard, fair, incorruptible, and knowledgeable, Judge Ward is about to introduce Pat to a new experience. "I find you guilty," thundered Judge Ward. This was the worst day of Pat's life. The judge said he would defer sentencing until he received a report from the case worker. In the meantime, the case worker would interview Pat, his family, and some friends before making a recommendation to the judge. Pat could be looking at six months in jail, a $500 fine, restitution, community service, and maybe more. He cannot believe all this happened because he hooked up with Al on the Fourth of July.

Pat decides to visit the public defender's office. Although public defenders in his state are required only to deal with felony cases, Pat hopes that maybe he can get some advice. A legal intern in the public defender's office tells him honesty is the best policy, and to cooperate with the case worker. He finds out that the case worker functions also as a probation officer. He does not trust this intern's advice. "Say nothing, it is your constitutional right," says Al.

After an uncooperative interview, Pat received a summons to Judge Ward's chambers. The case worker is there, too, and his report is thorough. It touches on Pat's past arrests, his uncooperativeness, and his denial of guilt. Judge Ward has a number of options: the fine, jail time, restitution probation, public service, or a new military-style training program designed to motivate and teach young offenders respect for authority. This is a federally sponsored program located on a nearby National Guard base. What would you do if you were Judge Ward?

Questions for Discussion

1. A "short, sharp shock" may sometimes be an effective deterrent, but is incarceration for minor offenses a cost-effective method of punishment from either an economic or a social point of view? What corrective measures are most likely to instill a sense of responsibility in this youthful offender? You have read the options. What do you think is the most effective way to adjudicate this case, and why? What would you hope for if you were the seventeen-year-old? If you were the seventeen-year-old's parents?
2. If Pat had no knowledge of the crime of stealing the beer, is he legally culpable? Is he morally culpable in some way? What should he do?
3. What corrective measures are most likely to install a sense of personal responsibility and moral awareness in this youthful offender?

4

"I Sorry, Officer"

You are a police officer assigned to patrol in an urban residential area. Your beat is a lower socioeconomic area comprised of housing projects, small stores, and warehouses. You are currently working the day shift.

While cruising down Elm Street, you routinely pull into a grocery store parking lot. Sometimes you are able to find stolen automobiles that have been abandoned in various public parking lots. As you begin to check a car with no license plates, you notice a small boy running between the parked cars. The boy appears to be attempting to hide from you. You get out of your patrol car and walk over to where the boy is hiding. You find the boy squatting behind one of the cars. He could be no more than seven or eight years old and is carefully guarding a large shopping bag he has in his possession.

You ask the boy where his mother is, thinking that a parent would not be far from such a small child. He quickly informs you that his mother is working at a factory two blocks away. The boy further explains that his father does not live with him and his mother anymore. He goes on to explain that his name is David and that he lives alone with his mother in a project several blocks away.

You look into the shopping bag and find that it contains radios, CD and casette-tape players, and other items commonly found in automobiles. You ask David where he got the contents of the bag and he tells you he found them. David is unable to explain to you where he found the items. You pick up the shopping bag, take David by the hand, and walk through the parking lot with him. You notice several cars with doors partially open and windows broken. Upon closer inspection, you find that they were apparently burglarized. Again, you ask David where he got the items in the shopping bag. David begins to cry and tells you he stole them from the cars in the parking lot.

You take David back to your patrol car and have him sit down in the front seat. By the way David is dressed you know he is poor. Sitting next to David in the car, you ask him what he was going to do with the stolen items. Still crying, he tells you about how he takes the stolen merchandise to a nearby high school and sells them to a teenage student.

Apparently this is not the first time David has stolen things. David only knows the teenage fence by his first name, Willie. He tells you that Willie usually gives him a couple of dollars for the stolen items. It is obvious that Willie has a good racket going, buying several hundred dollars worth of goods from kids like David for only a couple of dollars. Willie probably resells the items for ten or twenty times the money he gives the small, teary-eyed boy sitting in your cruiser. Seven-year-olds and teenagers! Your gut starts to ache as you wonder for a moment where it will stop, or if in fact it ever will.

David goes on to tell you that he only began stealing things a couple of weeks ago. He explains that he only wanted enough money to buy a birthday present for his mother next week. David says that his mother has not received a birthday present since his father left. He wants to buy his mother a new dress.

A lot of kids have lied to you before, but this time you believe what David is telling you. You feel sorry for him. Knowing that what action you take will have a lasting impression on the child makes you uncomfortable and frustrated. Generally, all you would have to do is turn David over to the juvenile authorities and let them handle the case. It sickens you to think about treating the child in a formal law-enforcement manner. You could wait until the owners of the property returned to their cars, give the items back to them, and take David home. But David needs to learn right from wrong. He needs so many things. You wonder how many other Davids are stealing for Willie. You buy David a Coke to buy yourself some time; you need to think. He looks up at you for an answer. Your cruiser's radio breaks the silence, "DWI on Elm Street. . . ."

Questions for Discussion

1. What should you do?
2. Could you effectively handle the situation by yourself? What options do you have?
3. The young boy could be an effective link into a serious burglary-larceny problem. What is the problem, and how could it be handled by the police?
4. Legally, your course of action can be simple—turn David over to the juvenile authorities. Ethically, can you become more involved in trying to divert this young boy from the system while maintaining your responsibilities as a police officer? If so, how?
5. What is the moral responsibility of society to boys like David? Why would he have to commit a crime to get what he needed?

5

Neighborhood Brat

You are a police officer assigned to the juvenile bureau and are presently responding to a request from a patrol officer to meet with you at a residence in the outskirts of the city.

As you pull up behind the patrol cruiser at the residence, a patrolman comes up to your car and tells you that he believes you should handle the situation inside. The patrolman explains that he answered a call to the Bakers' residence regarding an assault on the Bakers' twelve-year-old son. He states that the Bakers' next-door-neighbor, a Mr. Sutton, took a water hose and sprayed the Baker boy with it. Further explanation suggests that the Baker boy has been something of a troublemaker in the neighborhood. His previous escapades have included minor vandalism, fighting with other children, and generally being a nuisance to the neighborhood. In concluding his report, the patrolman laughs and tells you that he believes the boy probably "got off easy."

You approach the Baker house to talk with the parents. The boy's parents are visibly upset and insist that their son is very well mannered and that Mr. Sutton intentionally tried to harm their son. They further explain that their son has a cold and might well become seriously ill as a result of the incident. The Bakers are very angry and want to press charges against Mr. Sutton. Trying to be diplomatic, you advise the Bakers that you will talk with Mr. Sutton and will return shortly for further discussion with them.

You find Mr. Sutton in his back yard waxing his car. You introduce yourself and ask him what happened to the Baker boy. Mr. Sutton seems friendly and is quite cooperative in explaining his version of what happened. He contends that the Baker boy is always bothering people in the neighborhood by breaking windows, destroying gardens, and generally being a nuisance. Mr. Sutton goes on to explain that the boy came over while he was washing the car and started throwing dirt and mud on the car and running away. Finally, after warning the Bakers' son several times, he grabbed the boy and sprayed him with the water hose until he was soaking wet. After that the boy ran home crying. Mr. Sutton further informs you that despite many complaints from the neighborhood, the

Bakers treat their son as if he were always innocent and everyone else were lying.

Apparently, the Bakers are unable or unwilling to control their son. They appear to be overprotective and reinforce the child's behavior by not disciplining him. You are beginning to wonder whether the real problem is with the son or with his parents. Walking back to the Bakers' house, you must now decide what to tell them. It would be easier to advise the Bakers to take a warrant against Mr. Sutton and let the court handle the situation. On the other hand, the whole Baker family seems to need a different kind of help. You doubt they would be willing to commit themselves to family counseling, even if you tried to convince them it was needed. You mutter to yourself, "I am a police officer, not a psychologist."

You knock on the Bakers' front door, still undecided about what to tell them.

Questions for Discussion

1. Describe the ethical dilemma in which the officer finds himself. Should he talk with other neighbors about the Baker boy? Why or why not?
2. Since Mr. Sutton did actually grab the boy and spray him with water, it would constitute a physical assault by an adult upon a child, and Mr. Sutton has admitted to the "offense." Would the officer be in ethical violation if he ignored this "crime" and merely suggested that the Bakers sue Mr. Sutton civilly?
3. Could this matter be resolved in juvenile court? In civil court? Explain how either court could help the Bakers or be detrimental to them.
4. What is the ethical duty of police officers in a situation like this?
5. If the officer arrested Mr. Sutton or advised the Bakers to take out a warrant against Mr. Sutton, what would the court likely do in this situation? Would it be an ethical violation for the officer to advise Mr. Sutton how to defend his actions in court?

6

Zero Tolerance or Intolerance?

You are a school resource officer (SRO) assigned to Jackson High School. Your assignment as an SRO began three years ago when you were a "road deputy" with the Sheriff's Office. At first, you disliked the idea of being assigned to a school as a "guard" for high school "brats." The sheriff convinced you that this would be a good opportunity for the Sheriff's Office to gain the respect of teenagers in the community as well as establish rapport with educators. You reluctantly accepted the new post. It did have some benefits like weekends off and day shift only. The sheriff also told you that you could always go back "on the road" if you didn't like the assignment.

That was three years ago. Today, you are proud to represent law enforcement to the high schoolers and to be of service to the faculty. It has been a very rewarding three years. You have gotten to know most all the students and faculty on a personal level and have established rapport and respect with students and faculty alike. Sure, there have been some problems—fighting, cutting classes, larceny, and some other minor infractions. For the most part, though, they are a good bunch of kids, and the faculty members are supportive of your position. Students see you as a father figure and have frequently come to you for advice on everything from what the laws are on speeding to what to do about a cheating boyfriend. The students respect you and look up to you as a friend as well as a protector. It took a long time for you to gain that respect, and you are proud of your relationship with both the students and the faculty.

Jackson High has a new principal this year, Dr. Tedrow Taylor, who came here from a metropolitan area and has a doctorate in education from a very prestigious university. The school board was eager to accept his application, since he was a recognized leader in secondary education and wanted to relocate to a small rural area. Although Dr. Taylor seems pleasant enough, you have not had much chance to get acquainted with him. He strikes you as somewhat aloof, and he seems to talk down to his faculty—and to you. You have decided that is probably due to his big-city background and is nothing personal against you or the faculty. He does seem to have the ear of the school board, and he has been able to establish new rules and regulations at the school, such as zero tolerance on possession of drugs and weapons. He is now trying to create a new dress code for students. While there have been some complaints about his management style, parents have generally tended to support him.

"Officer Adkins, please report to the principal's office," the intercom blares during the lunch period. Your cell phone is also vibrating with a message from the principal's office. "Must be important," you think to yourself as you acknowledge the message on your cell phone. As you enter the lobby area of the principal's office, you see Steve Cunningham sitting on the couch with tears in his eyes. Steve is a senior with a near 4.0 average—a nice kid from a good home who has never been in trouble. He has a good chance of a full academic scholarship from the state university. "What are you doing here, Steve? You OK?" you ask.

"Guess you'd better ask the principal," Steve replies, trying to hold back tears. You can hear raised voices coming from the principal's office. You knock and enter to find Dr. Taylor in a heated argument with Mrs. Cunningham, Steve's mother. "What's going on here?" you ask.

"Officer Adkins, I'm afraid you may have to take this woman into custody. She has threatened me and is being disorderly on the campus. I want her removed immediately and taken to jail!" the principal demands.

"I never threatened this idiot, but I may give him a good punch if he doesn't start acting like a decent human being," Mrs. Cunningham replies. "He wants to kick my Steve out of school for drug possession. Do you know what drug he had? It was Tylenol—two capsules of Tylenol! I gave them to him this morning because he's been having stress-related headaches during the day. Now I know where the stress came from—this sorry excuse of a principal!" Mrs. Cunningham states angrily.

"OK, now calm down. Let me get this straight: you gave Steve a couple of Tylenol capsules to keep with him in case he got a headache today—right?" you ask.

"Yes, just two silly little Tylenol capsules, and this idiot acts as if I gave him heroin—like Steve's a drug dealer or something. Just how high can you get on a couple of Tylenol, Mr. Big-Shot Principal?" Mrs. Cunningham retorts to Dr. Taylor.

"Officer Adkins—I demand you take this woman into custody!" Dr. Taylor states.

"Dr. Taylor, just calm down for a minute. I don't work for you, I work for the sheriff of this county as a sworn law enforcement officer, and I haven't seen or heard anything yet that would warrant an arrest. Obviously, Mrs. Cunningham is upset, and I think we can resolve this matter calmly and without someone going to jail," you advise.

"If Steve gets kicked out of school for this, he'll never get that scholarship to the state university!" Mrs. Cunningham tearfully states, raising her voice.

"I told you that he could go to alternative school to complete his degree requirements here," Dr. Taylor interjects.

"Oh, that'll look real good to the scholarship committee—Steve in that alternative school with the rest of them delinquents. He won't have a chance of getting a scholarship with that on his record!" Mrs. Cunningham responds.

"Mrs. Cunningham—Susan. You know there is a zero tolerance rule about bringing drugs to school don't you?" you ask.

"Yes, but that doesn't mean Tylenol. That's for dope and prescription drugs and marijuana and illegal stuff. Not Tylenol."

"I know, but the rule states that you should have brought it in to the school nurse and had her dispense it—not allow Steve to keep possession of the pills," you try to explain.

"Well that's the stupidest rule I've ever heard of. I'll appeal this to the school board," Mrs. Cunningham replies, leaving the office in a huff, with her son in tow.

A couple of days later, you receive a call from Mrs. Cunningham. "Deputy Adkins, you've known us since Steve was a sophomore at Jackson. He looks up to you, and I do too. Would you please appear before the school board with us to appeal this decision to expel Steve?" Mrs. Cunningham asks.

If you agree to appear before the school board, you may be jeopardizing your position as the SRO at Jackson High. On the other hand, if you do not, your reputation with the other students at Jackson may suffer.

Questions for Discussion

1. What are the pros and cons of having a zero tolerance rule for drugs and weapons at public schools? Do you think there should be exceptions to the rule, such as in this case?
2. If you were Deputy Adkins, would you agree to appear before the school board? Assuming you decided to do so, what would you say to them?
3. If you were asked to develop a model policy about drugs and weapons at a public school, what would you include?

7

Cruisers

You are a patrol sergeant in a 116-officer police department. You are in charge of a patrol squad of nine officers in Zone 3, a patrol deployment area consisting mostly of commercial establishments such as a mall, numerous restaurants, two four-lane highways, and three shopping centers. Zone 3 is considered to be one of the busiest areas of the city, particularly on the 4:00 PM to 12:00 AM shift.

One of the shopping centers has become increasingly popular with local high school students as a place to cruise. The shopping center has a movie theatre that draws numerous young people on weekend evenings.

Shoppers and especially managers of many of the stores in the shopping center have turned in repeated complaints over the past few months. Traffic is overwhelming on weekends due to teenagers cruising around the shopping center. There have been several minor assault cases, and shoplifting charges have increased as well. Drug sale activity has also been suspected in the area.

Your watch commander, under orders from the chief of police, has asked you to keep a highly visible presence around the shopping center—the assumption being that a visible police presence will deter teenagers from cruising the area. You found out quickly that the presence of your officers in the same area as the teenagers did not deter the teens but increased the potential for hostility between your officers and the cruisers. Officers who questioned the presence of teenagers at the shopping center got the usual response, "What are we doing wrong?" The entrance and egress roadways in the shopping center are considered public thoroughfares in your state, so trespassing laws do not apply to cruisers.

Your officers have made several arrests of juvenile offenders for possession of alcohol, drugs, and shoplifting. However, the increase in arrests has not deterred the majority of the cruisers. You are aware that most of the young people cruising the shopping center are law-abiding kids, just out having fun. After all, it hasn't been that long since you went out cruising yourself as a high school student.

One day the watch commander calls you to headquarters.

"Roy, the chamber of commerce and the City Merchants' Association have pressured the city council on this cruising problem at Hillsdale Shopping Center. It seems the merchants are complaining that these kids are running off business and customers won't come in to shop with all the traffic there. The city council has passed a city ordinance against cruising which goes into effect the first of next month," Captain Adams explains.

"Captain, how are we going to enforce that? What do they define as 'cruising'?" you ask.

"Cruising is defined as any person operating a motor vehicle within a shopping or commercial area without the express intent of using the services of the establishments," the captain replies.

"Pretty vague—how do we know if they're cruising or using the establishments?" you continue.

"I don't know. Use your discretion. I guess let them cruise around the parking lot two or three times without parking, then write them up. Anyway, I want you and your officers to issue warning tickets this month just so the kids will know about the new law," Captain Adams advises.

As instructed, you and your officers wrote a number of warning tickets to the "regulars" over the following three weekends. Unfortunately, the warning tickets did not seem to have any substantial effect on the traffic. When the new law went into effect, you and your officers seemed to write citations pretty much nonstop for the next two weekends. The city judge, upset that he was not consulted about writing the new law and concerned about its constitutionality and vagueness, dismissed all "cruising" citations that came into his court. You too are concerned about the vagueness of the new law and about the police not having input on how the problem might be resolved. "The city council just passes some law to satisfy a few people and lets the police take the heat," you think to yourself.

As you suspected, problems began cropping up among the teenagers and your officers. Officers, attempting to enforce the new law, were ridiculed by the young people, called names—even spat on. This, in turn, caused your officers to become more hostile and aggressive with the teenagers. Arrests for disorderly conduct, failure to obey lawful orders, and even incidents of assault on officers were increasing. The merchants were also still complaining that the police were not doing a proper job of enforcing the law. Now, parents are complaining that officers have harassed and hassled their children without legal cause.

There have been several complaints, some justified, that officers wrote citations to people for cruising when, in fact, they were looking for a place to park in a crowded parking lot. One of your officers, a bit overzealous in his enforcement of the new law, even wrote up an elderly man and his wife for cruising when they went around the parking lot three times looking for a place to park close to a drug store. The teenagers are also blaming the police for enforcing the law, creating even poorer relations among your officers and the people they are supposed to serve.

Your watch commander calls you to headquarters just three weeks after the new law went into effect.

"Roy, the chief is supposed to present reasons why your officers have not enforced this cruising law at the next session of the city council. He called me demanding to know why we're not getting any results. I told him the judge wasn't enforcing the fine, so essentially there were no teeth in the law. He said that's the judge and city council's problem, not ours. Our problem is enforcing the law, not interpreting it. He's got the mayor on his back and numerous complaints from merchants, shoppers, and parents. He told me to come up with something to present to the city council. Now, Roy, you know more about what's going on out there than any of us. So I'm passing the buck on to you. This is your chance to come up with some solution to this problem. You've got three days to give me something I can take to the chief as a possible solution that he can present to city council."

You leave the captain's office despondent. The city council stirred this mess up, created an even greater problem, and *now* they're asking for police input. The merchants want a safe, comfortable shopping area. Shoppers do not want to fight teenage traffic, but the kids have rights too and really have nowhere else to go for fun. Unless you can get transferred out of Zone 3, you've got to come up with some workable solution before the situation gets out of hand at the shopping center. What are you going to tell the captain?

Questions for Discussion

1. List the rights each group has in this case: the merchants, the shoppers, the parents, and the teenagers. Which faction is more ethical in their approach to the problem—the police, the merchants complaining about the situation, the judge, or the city council? Which faction is less ethical in their approach to the problem?
2. What are some of the reasons for teenage cruising? Why are some places more popular than others? What problems exist for the teenagers and the police with cruising? What could the police do to ethically solve the immediate problem of cruising? What resources could they use and how?
3. Does the sergeant have an ethical obligation, beyond his legal duty, to attempt to resolve this situation in a way that would address both the rights of the teenagers and the concerns of the merchants?
4. If the news media were to write a story about this problem, how do you think the police would be portrayed?

8

Right Side of the Tracks—Wrong Side of the Law

You are a criminal investigator for a medium-sized sheriff's department serving a county population of nearly one million people. The sheriff, an elected official, usually keeps out of the business of law enforcement and would rather seek public attention and political recognition. The sheriff has indicated that he would like to seek a higher public office such as that of state representative in the near future. The chief deputy, Hal Owens, takes care of the daily business of running the sheriff's department.

You have received a call from the principal at one of the county's high schools regarding possible drug dealing, vandalism, and larcenies occurring in and around the school. You are scheduled to meet with Mr. Jaynes, the school principal, this morning.

"Good morning, Mr. Jaynes. I'm Detective Phil Anderson," you state as you walk into the principal's office.

"Yes, good morning. May I get you a cup of coffee?" Mr. Jaynes asks as he reaches for the coffee pot.

"That would be great, thanks. I take it black," you respond, sitting down next to the desk.

"I know you're busy so I'll get right to it. We've had some problems with vandalism and larcenies here at the school. I've also been suspicious of some of the students possibly being involved in drug dealing here on school grounds," Mr. Jaynes explains.

"Do you know who they are?" you ask, fumbling for your pen.

"Well, I don't have any proof, but I've made a list of those students I suspect. They hang out together," Mr. Jaynes states, handing you the list.

"I'm not too familiar with these names, except . . . is this Guy Edwards, Jr.—the state senator's son?" you ask, pointing to the list.

"Yes, it is. I know you must be surprised because of his father's position, but he's no angel here at the school. Those other kids are all from good families too. Bobby's father is a physician, Andy's is an attorney, and Gary's is president of the oil company here," Mr. Jaynes continues.

"Well, I am surprised these kids would get into anything as serious as drug dealing," you respond.

Later that day you decide to visit the district attorney to determine the best tactic in investigating the case.

"Yes, Phil, I see why you are concerned after reading this list of names," the DA states.

"I wanted to check with you to see how I should go about investigating these allegations," you respond.

"I'm not too concerned with the vandalism and petty larcenies at this time, but I am concerned about their involvement in selling drugs. I would suggest you stake out the school where they've been known to deal and get the usual evidence, photographs, and so on," the DA states.

Two weeks later, one of your undercover surveillance officers calls you to report that three of the boys had been arrested at the stakeout. One of the boys is the state senator's son, Guy Edwards, Jr.

"Caught them red-handed, Phil. Had coke, crack, and a bunch of Dilaudids they were selling like candy," the detective tells you while handing you the arrest reports.

"This is their first offense according to Juvenile Hall. They'll probably get off with probation and some community service work," you state.

The next day, Chief Deputy Owens calls you into his office.

"Phil, we've got a little problem with these kids on the dope charges. You know one of them is Senator Edwards's son. Senator Edwards and the sheriff are of the same political party and are good friends. The senator has been supporting the sheriff to run for state representative. You also may know that the DA is seeking the same office and is in a different party. Now, the DA wants to press this for all he can get politically. If he can get some bad publicity for Senator Edwards and the sheriff, it may help him during his campaign. The sheriff wants to know if you can help get these kids off as easy and as quickly as possible without a lot of media attention. Now, I'm not talking about doing something unethical here. If those boys are truly guilty, the sheriff says to throw the book at them. He can't afford a scandal either with something that looks like a cover-up," the chief explains.

"I understand. I'll see what I can do," you reply.

You have a meeting scheduled with Kevin Mitchell, a juvenile probation officer at Juvenile Hall.

"Kevin, what about these kids? Are they really rotten or do they have some hope?" you ask, referring to the arrest reports.

"I've never seen such a bunch of crybabies in my life. These kids are scared to death. You know, I've been in this business a long time and I know when I'm being conned. These kids have just gotten in with the wrong guy. They've all admitted to dealing drugs for this adult named Scooter Johnson, and they said they'd testify against him. All they were looking for was some excitement and I guess some attention," Kevin advises.

"So, they're willing to testify against their supplier, huh?" you acknowledge.

"I'll tell you something, Phil. That DA doesn't care about getting Johnson. All he's interested in is convicting these boys. He told me he's going for incarceration for these kids at Afton State Youth Center," Kevin advises.

"The kiddie prison?" you ask in a surprised manner.

"That's right. These kids don't need to go to Afton. I could handle them on probation and you could get their supplier on adult charges. If you will go to the judge with me, I believe we can convince him of that," Kevin explains.

You know that Kevin may be correct in his judgment. The boys would have a better chance on probation than incarcerated. You could satisfy the sheriff and get the adult supplier as well. However, you need a good working relation with the DA's office. The DA, even if his priorities are different, may be correct in pressing for incarceration. After all, the boys were dealing some hard drugs and may even be involved in other illegal activities. They may have even conned Kevin into believing their story. You remember when you were their age. You came up the hard way with no special privileges. Your father was a steelworker who believed in his country and the law. Besides, you never have cared much for crybabies. Still, this is their first offense, even if it is a rather serious one. What are you going to do?

Questions for Discussion

1. Should the detective go along with the juvenile probation officer and recommend probation? Explain the pros and cons of the decision.
2. Ethically, what should the detective do? What resources does the detective have that could help him act in the most ethical manner?
3. How do you think the detective's decision will affect his relations with the sheriff? The DA?
4. Are the DA and the sheriff in this case acting unethically? Which one's moral integrity seems to be more compromised? Why?
5. If the judge went along with the probation officer's and detective's recommendation to accept a plea in return for the children testifying against the adult drug dealer, over the objections of the DA, do you see any ethical problems with this arrangement? Why or why not?

9

A Loving Father?

You are a criminal investigator for a small police department serving a city of 78,000 people. You have worked as a criminal investigator for seven of your twelve years in the police department. Although crime in your city is not as serious as it would be in larger cities, you find there is plenty of work to do for a three-man detective division. June Wilson, an attractive Human Services social worker, has given you a telephone call.

"Pete, we need to get together and talk," June states.

"I'll chat with you anytime, anywhere," you state in a flirting manner.

"Now be nice, Pete. I'm serious. I've got a case you need to be involved in. I've got a 15-year-old girl and her 10-year-old sister in my office, and they're accusing their father of rape," June explains.

"Who did he rape, their mother?" you ask.

"Afraid not. He allegedly raped them," June responds.

"I'll be over in a few minutes," you advise.

As you enter June's office, you notice the two girls sitting on a couch in the reception area.

Exchanging hellos, June continues, "Hi, Pete. Just got off the phone with the juvenile court judge. She's sending over a court order to place the girls into protective custody at the Emergency Youth Shelter until this investigation is over."

"How did you find out about this rape thing?" you ask.

"The older girl told her school nurse what had happened and the nurse called me. I went over to the school and interviewed the girl briefly. Then we picked up her sister," June explains.

"When did they say their father raped them?" you ask.

"It wasn't a single act. Evidently this has been going on for some time with the older girl, Alice. Alice said her father began having intercourse with her when she was 11. Now she says her father is having intercourse on a regular basis with both her and her 10-year-old sister," June replies.

"This is sick. Do you think they're telling the truth?" you ask.

"I've talked with both of them together and separately, and I believe they're sincere. We'll have to go through the routine of taking their statements and videotaping their responses," June advises.

"Who's their father?" you ask.

"Name's Freddie Allen, resides at 1010 Elm Street with wife Eleanor," June states, reading from her notes.

"Is that the same Freddie Allen who teaches at the junior high school?"

"One and the same. He also is the choir leader at school, teaches Sunday school, and is the youth advisor at church," June responds.

"I'll need to talk with Mr. and Mrs. Allen," you advise.

"They're on their way here now," June replies.

A few minutes later the Allens arrive at June's office.

"What's going on here? Why are my kids down here?" Mr. Allen questions, angrily pushing his way into June's office, his wife following a few feet behind him.

"Sit down, Mr. Allen, Mrs. Allen. I'm Detective Rogers and this is Ms. Wilson. We need to ask you a few questions," you advise them in a calm, yet assertive voice.

"Look, all I want to know from you is why my kids are here and not in school," Mr. Allen repeats, his wife looking scared behind him.

You notice Mr. Allen is sweating profusely and appears to be on the verge of an emotional outburst.

"Mr. Allen, I must advise you of your constitutional rights . . ." you explain, verbally reading the Miranda warnings from your notebook.

"What's this all about? What am I supposed to have done?" Mr. Allen questions, getting more agitated and red-faced.

"Your daughters have accused you of having sexual intercourse with them on several occasions. A violation of state penal code number 245-23-454b," June explains, reading from her notes.

"Wait a minute. That's a lie. I've never touched them. Ask my wife; she'll tell you I've never touched them. I'll take a lie detector test. Bring them in here and let them say it to my face. They must be on drugs or something," Mr. Allen angrily interjects.

"Mr. Allen, I would suggest you contact your lawyer about this. The judge has issued a court order to place your daughters into protective custody until this is resolved. I personally haven't taken any statements from them yet. I'm not ready to ask you any specific questions until after I've interviewed your daughters," you explain.

"Freddie would never do anything like this. He's a good father and a good husband. He's a good provider. I don't know what we would do without him. My daughters are mistaken," Mrs. Allen adds with a shaky voice.

"I assure you, Mr. Allen, we will get to the bottom of this. We just needed to inform you of the current situation," you advise.

"Where are they? I'll get to the bottom of this. Let me talk with them," Mr. Allen demands.

"I can't let you do that at this time, Mr. Allen. You and your attorney will have a chance to cross-examine them later," you advise.

You proceed to make an appointment for Mr. Allen to come to your office tomorrow, and he leaves in a belligerent and frustrated manner. After talking with the two girls you learn that the 15-year-old reported her father because he started having intercourse with her sister. She always felt protective of her younger sister and felt she had to report her father before it was too late. You believe the girls are telling the truth but find there is little physical evidence to back up their story. It is basically their word against the word of their father and mother.

You remember past experiences where juveniles have lied about having sex with adults. Just last year you investigated a coach at the local high school for allegedly having molested some of the cheerleaders. He was acquitted. A terrible joke was played on him by some of the girls, but his career was ruined. No one ever believed he was really innocent after the accusations. You are aware that if the girls are telling the truth, the father is in need of help and might even molest the kids at school, if he hasn't already. You wonder how to best pursue the investigation and where to draw the line between arresting or not arresting.

Questions for Discussion

1. What are the legal guidelines for gathering evidence in incest and child sexual molestation cases? Neglect can be a gray area in terms of a judgment call. Is there a moral duty to these girls as well?
2. There is no physical evidence to support the girls' accusations. Should charges be placed against a person when there is no physical evidence—only accusations by a victim(s)? Would it be unethical to place charges against the father? Why or why not?
3. What are the characteristics of father–daughter incest and child sexual molesters in general?
4. Would you bring charges against Freddie Allen given the evidence at hand? How would you go about gathering evidence in this case?

10

Welcome Home?

You are a state trooper working interstate patrol near a metropolitan city, and you are on your way to meet a fellow trooper to run radar for the afternoon traffic. Just as you pass under a bridge, you see two subjects walking on your side of the interstate. As you look in the rearview mirror, you can tell that the subjects are both female, and one appears to be very young. You decide to turn at the next exit and see if the girls are in need of assistance. As you pass the girls on the opposite side of the highway, you notice the oldest girl trying to hitch a ride. You pull across the median strip in order to stop the girls.

The oldest girl appears to be twelve or thirteen years old, while the younger girl appears to be six or seven years old. When you ask the oldest girl to show some identification, she tells you she does not have any. You open the passenger door and ask the girls to sit in the front seat. Both girls appear to be scared, hungry, and tired. They apparently have no baggage, money, or even warm clothing.

You ask the girls where they are going, and they tell you they are looking for food. The oldest girl tells you her name is Jackie and her sister's name is Angie, but she will not tell what their last name is or where they are from. It seems the girls have run away from home. The youngest, Angie, has several small scars on her face. She has remained silent, letting her older sister do all the talking. One of Jackie's arms appears crooked, as though it had been previously broken and had healed without being properly set. Both girls are dirty and seem to be malnourished.

After some coaxing, the two sisters let you take them to a nearby burger joint, where they wolf down the food you order for them. With full stomachs, they seem more comfortable with you. Finally you ask Jackie if she and her sister are afraid to go home, and she tells you they are. In a choked voice, she explains that her parents beat her and Angie frequently, especially Angie. She goes on to tell you that she and her sister have been living in an abandoned warehouse for the last four days.

You call your supervisor on the radio and advise her that you have two juveniles in custody and will not be able to set up radar. You indicate that you are transporting the girls to the county juvenile advocacy center where a social worker can interview them.

When Jackie hears what your intentions are, she grows more fearful and tells you that she has been at the juvenile home before and that, after a short stay, they returned her and her sister to their parents. Jackie requests that you take them home rather than to the juvenile facility, adding that maybe their parents will not be too mad at them. You ask where she lives, and she tells you her home is about ten miles away. Advising headquarters that you are going to the girls' home, you proceed to Jackie's address to get a better assessment of the parents and the situation. Maybe you can do some good.

The parents live in a shabby house out in the country. You decide to talk with them first and leave the girls in your patrol car. Both parents are home watching television, and neither seems concerned that their daughters have been missing for four days. They ask what you want, and you explain to them that you have the girls outside in your cruiser. The mother indicates that she had been wondering when they would get tired of their "shenanigans" and return home. The father is still watching television and does not speak to you. The mother tells you to let the girls come on in and that she will handle them.

Questions for Discussion

1. Has the trooper done anything that might be construed as being unethical at this point?
2. What would be the most ethical decision the trooper could make regarding the girls? What would be the most unethical decision?
3. Sometimes police decisions are made based on assumptions about other institutions in the justice system. If the trooper believed that the advocacy center would simply turn the children back over to the parents, would he be unethical in leaving the children with the parents now? Why or why not?

11

A Conflict of Traditions

In your twelve years as a family court judge you have never had a case as disturbing as the one you are contemplating now. You must decide which parent will have custody of two children. Dwight and Amy Handel filed for divorce and both sued for the custody of the children, a boy seven years of age and a girl age five. Both of the children have indicated to you that they want to live with their mother because they are afraid of their father. One of the grounds for divorce was that the father was physically abusive to the mother as well as the children. Child Protective Services (CPS) investigations confirmed physical abuse by the father, and a CPS worker testified at the divorce hearing in support of the mother's case. On the other hand, the father testified that the mother had turned the kids against him by telling lies and that the abuse charges were made up. A child psychologist testified on behalf of the father, supporting that position.

Normally, this would not be a difficult case to decide. If both parents were supportive, then you would simply grant custody to the mother and father on an equal basis. However, you are not convinced that the father is not abusive. After all, the CPS report had been compiled as a result of a thorough investigation by social workers. However, that CPS report was based solely on interviews with the mother and the children. There was no physical evidence, such as bruising, found on the children.

What is even more disturbing is that the mother left the father, taking the two children with her, and moved into a friend's house. The father claims that the mother deserted him to live with her lesbian friend and that Amy and her "friend" are in a lesbian relationship. Amy openly admits that her relationship with her friend is homosexual and that they want to get married whenever the state recognizes same-sex marriages or unions. Yet no evidence other than the father's testimony was presented in court to indicate that the mother manipulated the children against their father. It seems clear that the children are truly afraid of their father and prefer to live with their mother.

You live in a state that is considered conservative, and your region is a small family-oriented community. People here have strong feelings about gay rights issues and this case will certainly be scrutinized, sensationalized, and even exploited by the news media. Your career as a judge may even be at stake, depending on how you decide this case. If you give custody of the children to the father, you may be putting the children at risk of further abuse—not to mention the charges of discrimination that would be leveled against you by gay rights organizations. If you give custody of the children to the mother, it may damage the children in terms of their social and emotional well-being, as the child psychologist testified. You would also be chastised by members of your community for giving custody to an openly homosexual couple. If you split custody equally between the father and the mother, you would face criticism from both sides of the issue and possibly put the children at even more risk.

"What is best for the children . . . what is best for the children," you keep murmuring to yourself. It is, after all, what is important in this case. Foster care is out of the question, since state law mandates that the family should be kept intact unless there is clear evidence that neither parent is capable of providing a nurturing home for the children. The grandparents are too old to take care of such young children, and there are no other family members willing to take custody.

"Judge Wilson, everyone is back in the courtroom ready to go," your secretary advises. It is time for you to render a decision.

Questions for Discussion

1. What would your decision be if you were the judge in this case? What are the reasons for your decision? What would be the probable consequences of your decision? How would your decision benefit the children?
2. If the location of this case were in a more liberal, metropolitan area, would this have an effect on your decision? Why?
3. If the decision you made would certainly result in your being removed as a judge, would you still make that decision? Why?
4. From what you have read about this case, which parent would be more likely to provide a loving, nurturing home for the children? Why?

12

Jihad Joey

Assistant District Attorney Harry Evans poured himself a cup of coffee. "Did you see the news last night?"

Todd Melborne nodded. "Yep. Looks like Rupert's pulling out all the stops."

Rupert Dillon, a four-term incumbent DA, had been defeated by upstart Todd Melborne who was, to make Dillon's defeat even more painful, a Democrat. Dillon intended to reclaim the DA's office in the upcoming election.

Harry read aloud a quote by Dillon at a local senior citizens' conference: "We cannot tolerate the liberal agenda in these dangerous times. Hakeem Zeitoun is a terrorist—plain and simple—and DA Melborne needs to remand him to adult criminal court to stand trial."

Harry folded the paper and laid it on the DA's desk. "A name like that is blood in the water for a shark like Rupert Dillon during election time."

Todd leaned back in his chair. "Of course, there is no mention that Hakeem's middle name is Joel and that everyone knows him as Joey Zeitoun. Rupert's playing to old folks' fears. Portraying a misguided 14-year-old as a full-blown terrorist is a cheap shot, even for Rupert."

Harry took a sip of coffee. "Still, it could gain traction. The kid did claim to several students that he knew some terrorists, and he did threaten to blow up the high school football stadium—it's in the police report. Some of the public will view that as a serious threat. You might need to do some saber rattling. With the election so close, you can't afford to be seen as soft on terrorism."

"I'm sure that's what Rupert would do if he were in my shoes," Todd replied. "Anything to win. The fact that the kid's father abandoned his mother and him when he was two years old or that the mother works two jobs to keep them afloat doesn't count."

"The kid did allegedly visit a terrorist website," Harry said as he refilled his coffee cup.

"True enough," the DA replied. "Of course, the reason we know about that is because his mother contacted a neighbor who is a police officer when her son told her about the website.

"He did threaten to blow up the football field," Harry interjected.

Todd threw a wadded-up piece of paper at the trash can. "He told one of his friends he would like to blow up the football field where three players who had been bullying him for the last two months were practicing. They've got half the school calling him Jihad Joey."

Harry drained the last of his coffee. "What you gonna do, Todd? Election's in three weeks."

The DA looked at his friend. "What I *could* do is, as you said, 'rattle my saber' and gain some political points. What I *should* do is divert Joey Zeitoun or, at least, recommend probation and counseling for him and his mother. And get the principal and guidance counselor at his school off their duffs to stop the troublemakers from harassing him."

Harry smiled at his boss. "Hmmm . . . the right thing. Feels good when you do it, not so good when you lose the election."

Questions for Discussion

1. Terrorism issues, real and imagined, are hot-button items during election time. Should the DA play both sides of the fence to get elected or, as he said it, "do the right thing"? If he does the right thing, what could be the consequences of his decision?
2. Does the school where Joey attends bear any responsibility for Joey's actions? What could they have done proactively that might have addressed the issues before they became a problem?
3. What role should our individual sense of right and wrong play along with our ability to separate fact from fiction when we hear claims like the one candidate Rupert Dillon made?

13

Guilty by Tattoo

"I know Eric has been a problem. That said, I've been seeing him daily for the last two weeks and he hasn't missed a single counseling session. Matter of fact, this week he has shown up early for each of his scheduled sessions."

Stu Morris looked at his second-year school counselor Scott Powell and thought to himself, "Still enthusiastic. Still believes every kid can be put on the right path. If only it were true."

The principal cleared his throat. "Scott, you are a good counselor—one of the best. But you know what Eric's track record is: one step forward and two or more steps backward. Last year, after he made the honor roll, he trashed the biology lab over Christmas break. His probation officer, Rory Devlin, has run out of patience and is more than willing to send him to the training school on my recommendation."

Scott leaned forward in his chair. "Look, Mr. Morris, Eric has screwed up plenty and you have already given him two chances more than he deserves. Still, we both know he is a bright young man who comes from a dysfunctional family. His dad's a deadbeat and his brother is serving a three-year prison sentence for burglary. If it wasn't for his mother, he would probably already be a lost cause. She's working two jobs and doing all she can to keep the family afloat. She's called me every week to check Eric's progress."

"You make some valid points," Stu replied, leaning back in his chair. "His mother seems like a good woman and there's no question that Eric is plenty intelligent, but then most sociopaths tend to be quite bright. For every prank he has pulled, Eric's conned his way out of two others. And then there's the matter of his tattoos, which I have a real problem with."

Scott shrugged. "There's not much we can do about that."

"True enough, counselor. I find his choice of tattoos offensive. I am even more concerned about the affect they could have on the other students. 'Love' across the knuckles on his right hand and 'hate' on his left, a machine gun on each forearm, and worst of all, the dashes across his throat with the words 'cut here.'"

Scott ran his hand through his hair. "Yeah, of all his tattoos, that one is definitely the worst. Eric told me that one was his brother's idea."

Stu popped a piece of gum in his mouth. "Of course, his brother is in prison and we are trying to run a high school."

"I know," Scott replied. "And I also know you have been more than patient with Eric. Maybe he deserves to be sent to the training school, but I wish you would give him one more chance. I really believe he and I are making progress. Seeing him graduate next year and maybe taking a shot at college sure would beat seeing him become a career criminal."

"That's a long shot, counselor."

Rising to leave, Scott smiled at his principal. "Sometimes long shots aim true."

Stu sighed, "Sometimes, but not often. It would be easier to give him another chance—but those tattoos!"

The two men shook hands. Alone in his office, Stu looked out of his window.

"I've got to tell Devlin something one way or the other. If it weren't for those damned tattoos."

Questions for Discussion

1. What role does personal bias play in the principal's perception of Eric?
2. Is the counselor in this cause being overly optimistic or naïve?
3. Eric's background and family environment have shaped who he is becoming, but does he also share responsibility for his own attitude and actions?
4. If you were the parent of a student who attended school with Eric, what would your perception of him be? As a parent, would you want him to be given another chance or to be sent off?
5. Legally, Eric's probation officer and the principal have adequate grounds for sending him to training school, but is it the right thing to do? Why or why not?

Bibliography

Law Enforcement

Bayley, D. H. (2002). Law enforcement and the rule of law: Is there a trade-off? *Criminology and Public Policy, 2*, 133–154.

Caldero, M. A., & Crank, J. P. (2010). *Police ethics: The corruption of noble cause* (3rd ed.). Cincinnati, OH: Anderson.

Catlin, D. W., & Maupin, J. R. (2004). A two-cohort study of the ethical orientations of state police officers. *Policing: An International Journal of Police Strategies and Management, 27*, 289–301.

Cordner, G. W., Scarborough, K. E., & Sheehan, R. (2010). *Police administration* (7th ed.). Cincinnati, OH: Anderson.

Crank, J. (2004). *Understanding police culture* (2nd ed.). Cincinnati, OH: Anderson.

Gaines, K. G., & Kappeler, V. E. (2008). *Policing in America* (6th ed.). Cincinnati, OH: Anderson.

Hanson, W. (1992). Ethics in law enforcement. *Ethics: Easier Said Than Done, 17*, 34–56.

Hayes, C. (2002). A consideration of the need for ethics training for police. *Police Journal, 75*, 322–329.

Herbert, S. (1996). Morality in law enforcement: Chasing "bad guys" with the Los Angeles Police Department. *Law and Society Review, 20*, 799–818.

Hooke, A. E. (1996). Training police in professional ethics. *Journal of Contemporary Criminal Justice, 12*, 264–276.

Illinois Criminal Justice Information Authority, Statistical Analysis Center. (1994). *Illinois municipal officers' perceptions of police ethics*. Chicago: Author.

Jones, J. R., & Carlson, D. P. (2004). *Reputable conduct: Ethical issues in policing and corrections* (2nd ed.). Upper Saddle River, NJ: Prentice-Hall.

Kappeler, V. E., & Gaines, L. K. (2003). *Community policing: A contemporary perspective* (2nd ed.). Cincinnati, OH: Anderson.

Longbottom, F., & van Kernbeek, J. (1999). Can reform of the police service be achieved through tertiary education? *Current Issues in Criminal Justice, 10*, 273–289.

MacIntyre, S., & Prenzler, T. (1999). The influence of gratuities and personal relationships on police use of discretion. *Policing and Society, 9*, 181–201.

Miller, L. S., & Braswell, M. C. (1992). Police perceptions of ethical decision-making: The ideal vs. the real. *American Journal of Police, 11*, 27–45.

Mills, A. (2003). Ethical decision making and policing: The challenge for police leadership. *Journal of Financial Crime, 10*, 331–335.

More, H. W., Wegener, W. F., & Miller, L. S. (2007). *Effective police supervision* (5th ed.). Cincinnati, OH: Anderson.

New York Law School Review Symposium. (1995). Police corruption, municipal corruption: Cures at what cost? *New York Law School Review, 40*, 1–188.

Newton, T. (1998). The place of ethics in investigative interviewing by police officers. *Howard Journal of Criminal Justice, 37*, 52–69.

O'Malley, T. J. (1997). Managing for ethics: A mandate for administrators. *FBI Law Enforcement Bulletin, 66*, 20–26.

Pollock, J. M., & Becker, R. F. (1995). Law enforcement ethics: Using officers' dilemmas as a teaching tool. *Journal of Criminal Justice Education, 6*, 1–20.

Prenzler, T., & Mackay, P. (1995). Police gratuities: What the public thinks. *Criminal Justice Ethics, 14*, 15–25.

Trautman, N. (1997). The National Law Enforcement Officer Disciplinary Research Project. *Law and Order, 45*, 34–37.

Walker, J. T., & Hemmens, C. (2008). *Legal guide for police: Constitutional issues* (8th ed.). Cincinnati, OH: Anderson.

Courts

American Bar Association. (2004). *Annotated model code of judicial conduct*. Chicago: Author.

Armstrong, K., & Possley, M. (2002, November 11). The verdict: Dishonor. *Chicago Tribune Reports*. Retrieved from http://www.ishires.com/dishonor.htm

Braswell, M., McCarthy, B., & McCarthy, B. (2011). *Justice, crime and ethics* (7th ed.). Cincinnati, OH: Anderson.

Cohen, E. (2002). Pure legal advocates and moral agents revisited: A reply to Memory and Rose. *Criminal Justice Ethics, 21*(1), 39–55.

Cohen, R. (2001, April 9). How they sleep at night: DAs turned defenders talk about their work. *American Lawyer: The Legal Intelligencer.*

Cole, D. (1999). *No equal justice*. New York: The Free Press.

Court, J. N. (2000). *The lawyers' book of ethics*. Kansas City, MO: Andrews McMeel.

Davis, M., & Elliston, F. (1986). *Ethics and the legal profession*. Buffalo, NY: Prometheus.

Fox, L. J. (1995). *Legal tender: A lawyer's guide to handling professional dilemmas*. Chicago: ABA.

Glendon, M. (1994). *A nation under lawyers*. New York: Farrar, Straus and Giroux.

Kaufman, K. (2003). *Legal ethics* (the West legal studies series). Clifton Park, NY: Thomson Delmar Learning.

Kennedy, A. (1999). Judicial ethics and the rule of law. USIS, Issues of Democracy. Retrieved from http://usinfo.state.gov/journals/itdhr/0999/ijde/kennedy.htm

Langford, C. M., & Zitrin, R. A. (2002). *Legal ethics in the practice of law* (2nd ed.) LexisNexis Matthew Bender Online.

Liebman, J. S., Gelman, A., Davies, G., Fagan, J., West, V., & Kiss, A. (2002). *A broken system, part II: Why there is so much error in capital cases, and what can be done about it*. Columbia Law School Publications. Retrieved from http://www2.law.columbia.edu/brokensystem2/report.pdf

Memory, J., & Rose, C. (2002). The attorney as moral agent: A critique of Cohen. *Criminal Justice Ethics, 21*(1), 28–39.

Olen, J., Van Camp, J., & Barry, V. (2004). *Applying ethics: A text with readings* (8th ed.). Belmont, CA: Wadsworth/Thomson Learning.

Pollock, J. (2005). Whatever happened to Atticus Finch? Lawyers as legal advocates and moral agents. In M. Braswell, B. McCarthy, & B. McCarthy (Eds.), *Justice, crime and ethics* (pp. 131–147). Cincinnati, OH: Anderson.

Pollock, J. (2008). *Ethical dilemmas and decisions in criminal justice* (6th ed.). Belmont, CA: Wadsworth.

Pollock, M. S. (1990). Prosecutorial ethics. *Institute for Psychological Therapies,* 2(4).

Radelet, M., Bedau, H., & Putnam, C. (1994). *In spite of innocence*. Boston: Northeastern University Press.

Rhode, D. L. (2003). *In the interests of justice: Reforming the legal profession*. New York: Oxford University Press.

Rhode, D. L. (2004). *Legal ethics* (university casebook series) (4th ed.). Westbury, NY: Foundation Press.

Shapiro, P. (2002). *Tangled loyalties: Conflict of interest in legal practice*. Ann Arbor: University of Michigan Press.

Spahn, T. E. (2004). Litigation ethics in the modern age. American Bar Association, *The Brief, 17*(2), 33.

Spence, G. (1989). *With justice for none*. New York: Penguin.

Van Camp, J. C. (2005). *Ethical issues in the courts* (2nd ed.). Belmont, CA: Wadsworth/Thomson Learning.

Wendel, W. B. (2006). Ethical lawyering in a morally dangerous world. *The Georgetown Journal of Legal Ethics, 1*(19).

Zitrin, R. A. (2006). *Legal ethics: Statutes and comparisons*. LexisNexis Matthew Bender Online.

Zitrin, R., & Langford, C. (1999). *The moral compass of the American lawyer.* New York: Ballantine Books.

Corrections

Bell, D. (1999). Ethical issues in the prevention of suicide in prison. *Australian and New Zealand Journal of Psychiatry, 33*, 723–728.

Bennett, J. (2001). Private prisons and public benefit: The impact and future of privately operated prisons. *Prison Service Journal, 135*, 40–43.

Braswell, M., Fuller, J., & Lozoff, B. (2001). *Corrections, peacemaking and restorative justice: Transforming individuals and institutions*. Cincinnati, OH: Anderson.

de Borst, E. J. (1992). Comment: Professionalism and loyalty in the implementation of prison policy. *International Criminal Justice Review, 2*, 119–128.

Del Carmen, R. V. (2005). *Briefs of leading cases in corrections* (4th ed.). Cincinnati, OH: Anderson.

Del Carmen, R. V., Vollum, S., Cheeseman, K., Frantzen, D., & San Miguel, C. (2008). *The death penalty: Constitutional issues, commentaries and case briefs* (2nd ed.). Cincinnati, OH: Anderson.

Gottfredson, S. D., & Gottfredson, D. M. (1985). Selective incapacitation? *The Annals, 478*, 135–149.

Lanza, K. L., Parker, K. F., & Thomas, C. W. (2000). The devil in the details: The case against the case study of private prisons, criminological research, and conflict of interest. *Crime and Delinquency, 46*, 92–136.

Latessa, E. J., & Allen, H. E. (2003). *Corrections in the community* (3rd ed.). Cincinnati, OH: Anderson.

Myers, L. B. (2000). Meeting correctional officers' needs: An ethical response to cultural differences. *Prison Journal, 80,* 184–209.

Nassi, A. J. (1975). Therapy of the absurd: A study of punishment and treatment in California prisons and the roles of psychiatrists and psychologists. *Corrective and Social Psychiatry and Journal of Behavior Technology Methods and Therapy, 21,* 21–27.

Palmer, J. W., & Palmer, S. E. (2004). *Constitutional rights of prisoners* (7th ed.). Cincinnati, OH: Anderson.

Pearlman, T. (1998). The ethics of the Texas death penalty and its impact on a prolonged appeals process. *Journal of the American Academy of Psychiatry and the Law, 26,* 655–660.

Radelet, M. L., & Barnard, G. W. (1988). Treating those found incompetent for execution: Ethical chaos with only one solution. *Bulletin of the American Academy of Psychiatry & the Law, 16,* 297–308.

Robinette, P. A., & Long, B. (1999). Is the segregation of HIV-positive inmates ethical? Yes; no. *Prison Journal, 79,* 101–118.

Rolland, M. (1997). *Descent into madness: An inmate's experience of the New Mexico state prison riot.* Cincinnati, OH: Anderson.

Schwartz, M. D., & Nurge, D. M. (2004). Capitalist punishment: Ethics and private prisons. *Critical Criminology, 12,* 133–156.

Silverman, M. (1993). Ethical issues in the field of probation. *International Journal of Offender Therapy and Comparative Criminology, 37,* 85–94.

Stohr, M. K., & Hemmens, C. (2000). Ethics in corrections. Special Issue. *Prison Journal, 80*(2).

Stohr, M. K., Hemmens, C., Kifer, M., & Schoeler, M. (2000). We know it, we just have to do it: Perceptions of ethical work in prisons and jails. *Prison Journal, 80,* 126–150.

Stone, A. A. (2002). Forensic ethics and capital punishment: Is there a special problem? *Journal of Forensic Psychiatry, 13,* 487–493.

Thomas, C. W. (1991). Prisoners' rights and correctional privatization: A legal and ethical analysis. *Business and Professional Ethics Journal, 10,* 3–45.

Thorne, F. C., & Forgays, D. G. (1973). Rehabilitation vs. security: The need for inmate protection in correctional institutions. *Journal of Community Psychology, 1,* 255–262.

Voorhis, P. V., Braswell, M., & Lester, D. (2009). *Correctional counseling and rehabilitation* (7th ed.). Cincinnati, OH: Anderson.

Weinstein, H. C. (2002). Ethics issues in security hospitals. *Behavioral Sciences and the Law, 20,* 443–461.

Whitehead, J. T., Pollock, J. M., & Braswell, M. C. (2003). *Exploring corrections in America* (2nd ed.). Cincinnati, OH: Anderson.

Juvenile Justice

Benekos, P. J., & Merlo, A. V. (2008). *Controversies in juvenile justice and delinquency.* Cincinnati, OH: Anderson.

Binder, A., Geis, G., & Bruce, D. D. (2001). *Juvenile delinquency: Historical, cultural and legal perspectives* (3rd ed.). Cincinnati, OH: Anderson.

Breda, C. S. (2003). Offender ethnicity and mental health service referrals from juvenile courts. *Criminal Justice and Behavior, 30*(6), 644–667.

Chesney-Lind, M. (2003). *The female offender: Girls, women, and crime* (2nd ed.). Thousand Oaks, CA: Sage.

Costello, J. C., & Jameson, E. J. (1987). Legal and ethical duties of health care professionals to incarcerated children. *Journal of Legal Medicine, 8*(2), 191–263.

Johnson, D., & Scheuble, L. K. (1991). Gender bias in the disposition of juvenile court referrals: The effects of time and location. *Criminology, 29*(4), 677–699.

Joseph, J. (1995). *Black youths, delinquency, and juvenile justice*. Westport, CT: Praeger.

Kempf, L. K., & Sample, L. L. (2000). Disparity based on sex: Is gender-specific treatment warranted? *Justice Quarterly, 17*(1), 89–128.

Leiber, M. J. (2002). Disproportionate minority confinement (DMC) of youth: An analysis of state and federal efforts to address the issue. *Crime and Delinquency, 48*(1), 3–45.

Leiber, M. J., & Mack, K. Y. (2003). The individual and joint effects of race, gender, and family status on juvenile justice decision making. *Journal of Research in Crime and Delinquency, 40*(1), 34–70.

Leiber, M. J., & Stairs, J. M. (1999). Race, contexts, and the use of intake diversion. *Journal of Research in Crime and Delinquency, 36*(1), 56–86.

Leiber, M. J., Woodrick, A. C., & Roudebush, E. M. (1995). Religion, discriminatory attitudes and the orientations of juvenile justice personnel: A research note. *Criminology, 33*(3), 431–449.

Leonard, K. K., Pope, C. E., & Feverherm, W. H. (Eds.). (1995). *Minorities in juvenile justice*. Thousand Oaks, CA: Sage.

Myers, D. L. (2003). The recidivism of violent youths in juvenile and adult court: A consideration of selection bias. *Youth Violence and Juvenile Justice, 1*(1), 79–101.

Ploeger, M. (1997). Youth employment and delinquency: Reconsidering a problematic relationship. *Criminology, 35*(4), 659–675.

Robinson, P. H. (2005). *Law without justice: Why criminal law doesn't give people what they deserve*. New York: Oxford University Press.

Singer, S. I. (1997). *Recriminalizing delinquency: Violent juvenile crime and juvenile justice reform*. Cambridge, MA: Cambridge University Press.

Talley, C. T., Rajack-Talley, T., & Tewksbury, R. (2005). Knowledge and perceptions of juvenile justice officials about selection bias. *Journal of Criminal Justice, 33*(1), 67–75.

Tanenhaus, D. S. (2004). *Juvenile justice in the making*. New York: Oxford University Press.

Walgrave, L. (1995). Restorative justice for juveniles: Just a technique or a fully fledged alternative? *Howard Journal of Criminal Justice, 34*(3), 228–249.

Whitehead, J. T., & Lab, S. P. (2004). *Juvenile justice: An introduction* (4th ed.). Cincinnati, OH: Anderson.

Wolfson, M., & Hourigan, M. (1997). Unintended consequences and professional ethics: Criminalization of alcohol and tobacco use by youth and young adults. *Addiction, 92*(9), 1159–1164.